BLUE GRIT

BLUE GRIT
THE JOHN BROWN STORY

JOHN BROWN
with DEREK WATSON

FOREWORD BY IAN DURRANT
and ALLY McCOIST

MAINSTREAM
PUBLISHING
EDINBURGH AND LONDON

First published in Great Britain in 1995 by
MAINSTREAM PUBLISHING COMPANY (EDINBURGH)
LTD
7 Albany Street
Edinburgh EH1 3UG

ISBN 1 85158 822 1

A catalogue record for this book is available from the British
Library
Printed by Butler & Tanner Ltd., Frome

For Lizzie and Joanne

Contents

Foreword	by Ian Durrant and Ally McCoist	9
Chapter One	Treble Yell	15
Chapter Two	Just Champion	29
Chapter Three	Accie Days	43
Chapter Four	Opportunity Knox	53
Chapter Five	Not a Billy Bhoy	63
Chapter Six	Blue Heaven	67
Chapter Seven	Hearts Attack	75
Chapter Eight	The Famous Five	81
Chapter Nine	Bombed Out	93
Chapter Ten	Durranty	101
Chapter Eleven	Blue Grit	109
Chapter Twelve	The Gaffers	117
Chapter Thirteen	Scots on the Rox	131
Chapter Fourteen	Final Countdown	137
Chapter Fifteen	The Foreign Legion	143
Chapter Sixteen	Standing Count	155
Chapter Seventeen	Simply the Best	159
Chapter Eighteen	The Coach	169

Foreword

Ian Durrant and Ally McCoist

Durrant: The first thing I'd like to say about John Brown is . . . I still haven't forgiven him for diving for a penalty when he scored a hat-trick against Rangers. The second is, how come Coisty and I gubbed his Dundee mob twice just before he arrived and Souness still signed him?

I first came across Bomber when he played for Hamilton Accies and I'd go and watch them in the odd game. A few years later I found myself playing against him midfield on several occasions. One game that sticks in my memory was the match we lost 3–2 at Dens Park with Bomber scoring a hat-trick. He was in a different class that day, even though I haven't forgotten that penalty incident.

That red hair was misleading but I soon found out that Bomber was a Rangers man and even though he was playing for the opposition we used to talk to each other on the park. We had a couple of tussles but at that time I weighed about five stones, so it wasn't much of a contest. Just before he signed for us (I was up to about nine stones by then) we beat them twice in a short space of time. In the first match the score was 2–0, but it could have been six, and it was a similar story the second time around. I had to bring him out of my back pocket so Souness could sign him. To be serious for a moment, with million-pound signings the norm in football these days, at £350,000 Bomber was the steal of the century in terms of what he's done for the club. He's also the most sincere man I've ever met in football. A spade's a spade with

Bomber. It doesn't matter to him if you're the best player in the world or a youngster, he'll still treat you the same way.

After he signed for us he made his Old Firm début in the 5–1 game and I think he'd be the first to admit that he was absolutely knackered that day. He was the whitest person I've ever seen on a football pitch and the last ten minutes were a daze for him which we all found hysterical. I was sitting on the terraces after an injury when he scored his first Old Firm goal. He jumped the billboards to celebrate, which just showed how much that moment meant to him. He signed as a midfielder, but he always had those defensive qualities as well as the ability to get a few goals.

When I was out injured for a long period I used to stay at Bomber's a lot; I'd go over and have dinner with him and his wife, Diana. They helped me get through a tough time, and I've got to thank them for that.

Anyway, that's the kind bit of this foreword finished, over to you, Coisty.

McCoist: Act 1, scene 1: early Seventies. Blantyre High School, with super striker John Brown, versus Hunter High, with the East Kilbride side skippered by one A. McCoist, a talented sweeper, with chunky midfield maestro Andy Knox also in the side for a cup final played at Blantyre Vics ground. Midway through the first half, crowd trouble developed, police arrived, and play was held up as kids spilled on to the park, but when the dust had settled Hunter High held on to a 1–1 draw. With scorers Knox, from a 20-yard free kick, and Brown. We don't really want to talk about the replay, but Blantyre won 4–1.

Act 4, scene 20: New York, present day. Brown and McCoist (MBE) are in the States as part of a visitation to supporters clubs along with Ibrox PR man John Greig (also MBE). After three hectic days in the Big Apple, we've had our fill and we're right down to the core when we decide to go for a meal on our last night. Our hotel commissionaire points us in the direction of a steakhouse serving the finest fillets your US buck can buy. Presently, two of the biggest Charlie Drakes in the world arrive (we didn't know whether to climb them or eat them) and as I tuck into my Friesian and fries I notice Bomber's eyes closing before he eventually falls asleep . . . face down on his steak. 'Say, buddy, ain't you gonna wake your friend up?' asks the guy at the next table. 'Nope, this is the first peace and quiet I've had in three days,' I told him.

I'm sorry, Bomber, but I've got to tell this one as well. When we moved on to Las Vegas to meet supporters there, we stayed at the biggest hotel I've ever been in. It had everything, including a full-size electronically controlled model, which spoke, laughed and told jokes. I swear that I came down from my room to find Bomber enjoying a Budweiser or two, getting a round in for himself and this 'guy' at the bar. 'What are you up to?' I asked him. 'Nothing much, Coisty,' he told me. 'Just having a few quiet drinks with this lad here,' as his new chum threw back his head and went 'ho, ho, ho'. Honest!

On a more serious note, I've got to agree with Durranty and say John Brown is one of the greatest Rangers players with whom I've ever been on a park. He would definitely be in my greatest- ever Rangers team because he epitomises everything that's good about a Rangers player. His attitude is the same in every game – 100 per cent. And in the modern day when there is a lot of criticism levelled at players for being too money orientated and not thinking about the game and the club they play with, nobody could charge John Brown with that. He's one man who, throughout my career, has been an example to one and all.

Now I've bummed him up a bit, I have to say that he was nearly solely responsible for ending my Rangers career. He scored the only goal of the game in a cup tie at Ibrox when I missed chance after chance . . .

Durrant: Whose book is this, Bomber's or yours?

McCoist: As I was saying, John came off the park put his arm around me and tried to cheer me up. Neither of us could believe what had happened. We've known each other for nearly 20 years and played against each other as well as in the same team and I look on him as a brother and a friend.

But as Durranty has already said, how he ended up at Ibrox is a mystery because he and Jimmy Smith marked myself and Ian at Ibrox just before he signed and it was the biggest doing in the history of Rangers–Dundee matches. We turned them so often that night I'm sure one of them struck oil. We had to get Red Adair out for Bomber after I'd screwed him into the ground!

Durrant: You're right, I don't know what the Gaffer saw in him. He must have been drunk in the stand that night. Two weeks later, to our astonishment, the boss signed him.

McCoist: He must have improved though, and now Bomber will go down as one of the greatest players never to be capped for Scotland, which is a mystery and a travesty as far as I'm concerned.

Durrant: In the Champions League season, Marseille were probably the best side in Europe on their day and his two performances against them were unbelievable. Goughie was captain, but having Bomber on the pitch was like having a second skipper. That season he had to be the best centre-half in Britain.

McCoist: And when we played Brugge in Belgium I thought he must have had a twin. He took them on himself in the second half. One minute he was making a tackle at the back, the next he was popping up in the box to have a shot on goal.

Durrant: Even now his attitude is second to none. Recently, I played with him in the reserves and he strolled through the game. He's still one of the best centre-halves at the club and that frightening motivation he's got is still there. He's now in the twilight of his career but you can still see that gleam in his eyes and the hunger he has for the game. He's also one of the best pros I've ever met. You get some players calling off with niggly injuries, but

Bomber's always there. I can't pay him too high an accolade – he's one of the best I've played with.

McCoist: On the down side, I have to say he's a real bandit on the golf course. He's a very good golfer who plays off a ridiculously high handicap and takes a lot of money from me. And I also have to mention that there's a side to John Brown which a lot of people don't see – the family man. One thing that's very apparent is his love for his family and when you see him with Diana, Lauren and Megan you really appreciate how precious they are to him.

I value his friendship very highly. There's not a lot of people of whom I could put my hand on my heart and say I trust 100 per cent and could rely on, but John's one of them.

Durrant: I'd agree with that, but I'd like to finish by saying that we're now making the arrangements for the players' Christmas party, to which Bomber can't come because he's now on the coaching staff and will have to go to their do instead. If you've shelled out for a copy of this book and you're reading this, Bomber, don't worry, we'll tell you all about it when we're next in the reserves and we'll keep you a copy of the programme that Ally's mate, Charlie, produces for the night . . .

McCoist: And after a foreword like this, you owe us both a good few beers. Cheers, Bomber, all the best.

Chapter One

Treble Yell

Ritchie, Shearer, Caldow, Greig, McKinnon, Baxter, Henderson, McMillan, Miller, Brand, Wilson . . . A legendary Rangers line-up, and names which every Rangers fan, myself included, can still rattle off. A team which contained some of the Ibrox greats . . . among them the legendary Jim Baxter. This was an Ibrox side which captured the coveted Treble of League, League Cup and Scottish Cup for only the second time in 1964 to join the famous 1948 Iron Curtain side led by Jock 'Tiger' Shaw – the team which swept to the Gers' first clean sweep. Nearly 30 years on, it was Goram, McPherson, Gough, Brown, Robertson, Murray, Ferguson, McCall, Durrant, Hateley and Huistra, as Walter Smith led us to the club's fifth Treble triumph. We probably didn't realise it at the time but on that sunny May afternoon – at Parkhead of all places – we were about to join the legends.

I had watched from the terracings as Jock Wallace led the Light Blues to *two* Trebles in 1976 and 1978. And what made our victory even sweeter that day as we clinched the Scottish Cup with a 2–1 victory over Aberdeen, was erasing the knowledge that we had blown an earlier Treble chance in 1989. It's an afternoon I'd rather forget . . . one that few of us who played at Hampden against Celtic that day *can* blank out. A throw-in that never was – a rare mistake from Gary Stevens and Celtic snatched the Scottish Cup and our Treble chances.

Four years on there was no way we were going to blow it for a second time. After that downer, we always felt we had the squad to do it. But you also need a bit of luck, something that was missing from that particular final, but not, thankfully, from our Cup run in 1992–93.

People forget that until 1992, when we beat Airdrie 2–1, we were also-rans in the Scottish Cup. It had been 11 years since a Rangers captain had lifted the cup at Hampden and in between times there had been some shocks, like our first round exit against Hamilton. But from the moment I scored my first Old Firm goal in the Ne'erday derby at Parkhead in January 1992, we didn't look back and from then until the end of our Treble-winning season I had the greatest 18 months of my career. As the song says, 'There's not a team like the Glasgow Rangers' and that's certainly true in terms of team spirit – a vital ingredient of our Treble triumph.

The biggest factors in that success were that camaraderie and continuity – the fact that we used almost the same squad throughout. There weren't a great deal of injuries and playing together for a year and half without chopping and changing the team every week helped us play some great football. The boys all got on well together socially and there was a bond between us that certainly didn't exist at other clubs. We're always out for lunch together, or going for a few beers; not all dressing-rooms are as happy.

Gordon Durie has told me that during his time at Spurs the only time the players saw each other was at training or on a Saturday; they never went out together. And before Brian Laudrup signed for us after an unsettled period in Italy with AC Milan, the first question he asked Mark Hateley was whether or not the players socialised together. Thankfully, Mark was able to set him straight and report that occasionally we enjoyed the odd shandy together.

At Ibrox it worked well for us. We had a great time, there's no denying that, but we knew when to draw the line between work, rest and play. (Well . . . sometimes!)

People are always quick to criticise if they see you having a few beers or enjoying yourself, especially after a defeat, but the fact that we knew each other so well meant we would work hard for each other on the pitch. And not having the injuries we had suffered from in previous and successive seasons was also vital. Even when we had a few knocks here and there, the nucleus of the side was virtually the same.

I have to say it was the most satisfying period yet for me. I was injury-free and playing what I thought was the best football of my career. In the summer after the Double-winning season I was busy at an SFA coaching course at Largs a week before pre-season training in Italy. That was great for my fitness level and helped keep me in shape throughout the season.

The other vital ingredient in our success over that period was that eight or nine of the team were playing exceptionally well every week. Normally, you would be happy with half a dozen performing that way. When we did have to make changes we knew we could rely on younger lads like Steven Pressley, Neil Murray, Gary McSwegan, Stephen Watson and David Hagen. We had a midfield core of Stuart McCall and Ian Ferguson, two guys who make things a lot easier for any defence. Stuart's work-rate is incredible, but a lot of credit goes to Fergie. They both tackle back and win the ball before it gets near the danger area, as well as posing a great threat at the other end. Since he signed for us from St Mirren in a million-pound deal, Fergie's suffered more than most from illness and injury. But that year he had a pre-season under his belt, something that he'd missed for a few years, and that definitely had an effect. When you're chasing your fitness, it's a hell of a task to produce the goods. In the previous season, Fergie had missed out on the Scottish Cup final because of a lack of fitness and form and thought he would be out the door, but, during the 1992–93 season, Fergie was fresh and strong.

What a turnaround! A year down the line, from thinking he'd be transferred, he found himself playing for one of Rangers' best-ever teams in one of the most successful periods in their history!

The first part of the Treble is, of course, the League Cup. And although in recent years there has been talk of scrapping it because of the congested fixture list, I for one would hate that. Not only has it been an enormously successful competition for Rangers, who've captured the trophy on 19 occasions before 1995, it was also the first medal yours truly won in senior football – the dramatic 1988 final against Aberdeen.

In fact, during my time at Ibrox I've played in four finals and won three of them. My runners-up medal would have come against Aberdeen in 1989, only I was so disappointed that I didn't even go up the Hampden steps to pick it up. That was nearly as big a disappointment as being denied the chance of a clean sweep of domestic honours by Hibs in the 1991–92 season as Keith Wright beat his old team-mate, Andy Goram, to notch the only goal of the game in the semi-final. Afterwards Andy joked that if he had stayed at Easter Road he would have won a medal. This prompted Ally McCoist to retort that if Andy had stayed at Easter Road *he* would have won a medal!

The following season, we headed for Hampden on the Sunday after we had beaten Leeds in the European Cup first-leg tie at Ibrox. The atmosphere at Ibrox that night for the European match was one of the best I can remember, but it seemed to take a lot out of the fans as they were a bit quieter at the start of the final. As the game went on, we got stronger and won it in extra time. Our will to win carried us through that day and in the League, where other teams were always waiting for us to strike back, even if they went ahead. Our determination was a very important factor throughout the season.

From his point of view, the way Aberdeen defender Gary Smith deflected the ball into his own net was very unfortunate, but we weren't complaining and, really, after grabbing the opener through Stuart McCall, and suffering a sickening equaliser from Duncan Shearer, it was just a matter of time before we hit back.

Bringing the first cup of the season into the Ibrox Trophy Room was a great boost, as was qualifying for the Champions League with our famous victory at Elland Road in the rematch against Leeds in November. We had proved ourselves to be winners already. We had risen to the big occasion and we were looking forward to every single game.

Preparation, of course, was vital. And we geared up for competition at highest level of European and domestic football in the most unlikely of settings – our local caff! Much was made during Graeme Souness's regime of the introduction of a high-carbohydrate pasta diet. But under Walter Smith and Archie Knox bacon butties were back on the menu, along with our usual healthy grub.

I would say that it was probably the manager and the backroom team's easiest year in terms of preparation! People who subscribe to the view that professional football players should work nine-to-five and be able to peak at the top of their form every day of the week will probably frown on the Gaffer's off-the-field tactics, but they were just as successful as the ones he employed on the pitch. We were all fit, playing well and, as far as everyone was concerned, all that mattered was producing the goods on a Wednesday or Saturday.

At that time we were hardly training because we were playing so many games. On the day before big games (well, they're all big games if you play for Rangers) we could be found down Antonio's tucking into pie and beans, fritters, and ice-cream sodas. We simply saved our legs for the games and ran off our junk food with a nice game of five-a-sides – that was as strenuous as it got! But when you consider that I played maybe sixty games and our international players were lucky if they had three free midweeks over a ten-month period, then you can appreciate just how thankful we were for that approach.

Fans sometimes wonder how they manage to work a five- or six-day week, doing a job with much longer hours. But what they forget is that footballers are involved in a contact sport and pick up the inevitable knocks which reduce their effectiveness and take a few days, sometimes longer, to recover from. That year, for example, some of the team played in spite of niggling injuries. They knew that, if they told the manager they weren't fit, someone else could come in and, if they did a good job, keep them out of the team. Scott Nisbet, who has now had to retire from the game, played with the injury problems which eventually forced him to chuck it. That was very sad for him, but he played through a lot of pain just to make the most of the chance – all of us sensed what a great season it could turn out to be.

Getting the first silverware of the season gives the whole place a lift – players, management and all the staff at Ibrox. Going back to the stadium for a party with everyone from the chairman to the cleaners was great and the supporters up and down the country have a ball too. Like us, they knew that we were the only team in the country with the chance of the Treble and at that point we could feel that if there was ever going to be a season to do it, this would be the one. We knew that with Europe to contend with as well it would be even more difficult. But as well as our Cup triumph, we were doing well in the League and putting together what would eventually be a 44-unbeaten-game run, sparked off by a 4–3 defeat against Dundee at Dens Park at the start of the season. After all those European ties, it was quite an amazing feat, and a lot of it was down to the players' attitude and character.

The banter and spirit in the dressing-room, with guys like Ally McCoist, Ian Durrant and Ian Ferguson, who's got a really dry sense of humour, and David Robertson who's got a *weird* sense of humour, kept us going. Robbo, being an Aberdonian, has a different way of looking at things, but he can come out with one-liners which can reduce the dressing-room to tears. That kind of thing kept us all going through the good and bad.

Ibrox is a great place to go every morning. You get paid to do a job which you love, for a team you love, and even the foreign players who come to the club realise after a wee while what it's all about. They've got the same feel for the place as the rest us. That kind of spirit and team-work came into its own on the park. On so many occasions we would go one down and then hit back. It was as if we were waiting for the challenge and then responding to it. But we were on an unbeaten run and not one of us was willing to give it up.

As I've said, beating Leeds and qualifying for the inaugural Champions League in what was the biggest game of the season in a season with so many massive games gave us a tremendous boost.

20

But a result like that at Dens Park was something few would have predicted after just the third game of the League campaign. Seven-goal thrillers are great for TV executives, sportswriters and of course the fans . . . But when you're on the end of a 4–3 defeat against a newly promoted side in the third game of the season, you have to admit it's not one of the highlights of your career. However, that defeat against Dundee probably did us more good than harm. Dens Park boss Simon Stainrod slaughtered us that day and we were due it.

But the old saying about the Premier Division being a marathon not a sprint isn't far off the mark – we went on to win the League and they were relegated, which even if we'd have known it at the time wouldn't have been much comfort. The Gaffer gave us a real rollicking and from then on there was a bit more steel in our performances. We were determined not to let it happen again – to a man we were embarrassed. I can remember reading a newspaper article before the game, warning that as they were newly promoted and playing against the champions Dundee would be on a high. And if we'd have played them later in the season after they'd had a few more Premier games they might have been less hungry for a result.

From there, however, we went from strength to strength. It was maybe a good thing that it happened so early as it set us up for that run and prepared us for Europe too.

In those situations the Gaffer isn't Souness, but if you get on the wrong side of him you won't know what's hit you. Walter's not as wild as Graeme, but when he does raise his voice you listen.

We got back on the rails after that Dens disappointment and soon we faced Aberdeen, who were to be our main challengers again, which meant that every time we played them there was always more riding on the outcome than just two points. For them to finish second to us three times that season must have totally devastated them, especially as in any other year their displays would probably have won them a couple of trophies.

The first game between the sides at Ibrox was possibly our best second-half performance of the season, with some breathtaking football and great goals. Roy Aitken, who was player/coach at the time, put them ahead with a 25-yard volley which was a real sickener. But we fought back with strikes from Ian Durrant, Coisty and Alexei Mikhailitchenko. The football was excellent and it was a good day to blitz them. The Dons had a good side that season and they kept getting decent results, but we carried on getting better ones.

Games against Aberdeen are even more physically demanding than Old Firm matches. In recent seasons they've always been just behind us and you always have to work hard to get a result up there, graft and take some pressure. But Europe had got us into the habit of keeping our nerve and concentration for 90 minutes and waiting for a break – inevitably we got one.

So winning at home was important, but it was even more vital to get a decent result at Pittodrie. After defeating them in the League Cup final, a few days after our Elland Road exploits, we went on to grab both points up there in February, thanks to a vintage header from Mark Hateley. Andy Goram was brilliant that night and we soaked up some pressure before grabbing a late winner. The critics would probably say 'lucky Rangers' but you need more than luck for a 44-unbeaten-game run. That was a crucial result as it gave us a nice cushion. If they had won it would have reduced our lead and put them right back in the hunt. That would have made us a bit more apprehensive, made us approach games differently, with our confidence down. That all has a knock-on effect and you start making mistakes.

In our next encounter Ian Ferguson and Ally gave us the goals which all but wrapped up the title. But it wasn't just the Dons who were on the receiving end – going to Tannadice in September and thumping Dundee United 4–0, with Piet Huistra grabbing two goals, boosted our confidence, and Durranty's winner at Parkhead immediately after our Elland Road clash was also vital.

Our unbeaten run came to an end at Parkhead just days after we beat Brugge 2–1 at home in the Champions League and I personally felt even worse about it as I had been made captain for the day. We were 2–0 down when Mark pulled one back and he had a great chance to level it in the last few minutes. But even though we felt bad about losing our unbeaten run, it helped that on the day, because of our European efforts, our fans couldn't have cared and they sang their hearts out regardless. That was the only big game we lost that season, but the run had to end sometime, although we would have preferred to avoid it happening against our oldest rivals.

In the event, six weeks later Gary McSwegan was the man who wrapped up the title for us at Broomfield, but towards the end of the season a lot of youngsters did well for us. Neil Murray was exceptional, particularly in Europe where his finest game was away to Brugge. He had a superb game which was the type of performance you would expect from a senior player, not a rookie. Another outstanding asset that year was definitely Ian Durrant. He makes great runs and holds the ball up well and he's also got a great football brain and loves the big stage. Unfortunately, he was to miss out on our Broomfield bash, as the manager rested him for the Cup final.

He wasn't the only one who was down in the mouth about missing out. Sad moments were few and far between that year, but there was a real downer just before we clinched the title in May when Coisty broke his leg playing for Scotland against Portugal shortly before. When you consider that Scotland were losing 5–0 at the time it made it even worse. Ally was going for a shot, the defender blocked him and his season was over. He was sitting on the 49-goal mark, he knew the sort of season we were having and he would have scored far more if he hadn't missed those five games at the end of the campaign.

I was even more gutted for him when I found out that he couldn't even come and watch us against Airdrie as the Doc had banned him. Knowing he couldn't be there to watch us claim the title must have hurt more than anything, especially as we were about to clinch the second part of the Treble. It must have broken his heart. We won it, thanks to a Gary McSwegan goal which earned him his place in the history books, and the celebrations started. I still had a lump in my throat until I spotted a full-size cardboard cut-out of Coisty in the crowd. Typically he still found his way into the celebration pics and almost stole the show!

Missing out on the Scottish Cup final against Aberdeen must have been just as bad. For someone who had done so much for his team that season with all the vital and spectacular goals he scored and all the important matches he helped us win, it was a real sickener. I don't know how I would have coped, but, on the surface, Ally was different class – underneath he must have been really cut up. That's a side to him that people rarely see and it does him credit that he hardly ever shows it. He's got a smile for everyone.

It was a big blow for us, too, but it made us even more determined to carry on and hopefully give him a bit of credit by winning the Treble. Airdrie was a special day. The fans were superb on our lap of honour and I remember spotting my dad and some friends in the stadium. I also nearly caused a riot in our house when my wife Diana heard on the radio that I had taken off my jersey and handed it over to a blonde in the crowd. But fortunately it was our babysitter, Morven, and Diana forgave me.

That evening was everything you could want it to be. I returned to my roots in Blantyre at the Union Jack Club. I used to catch the Rangers supporters bus from there when I was younger and nowadays I win their Player of the Year award no matter how badly I play. I took Ally along and Fergie. Coisty was on crutches and the punters *loved* him. The capacity in the hall was about 150, but my mate Big Stan's dad was on the door and he must have let at least 350 in (I'm still waiting for my cut), so you couldn't breathe in the place. To go there after winning the League was fantastic and even on crutches Coisty was brilliant – they're still talking about that night down Blantyre way. We then headed off into town with a couple of my mates and a case of champagne the supporters club had kindly provided and the celebrations continued.

Apart from the atmosphere, the thing that gave me the most pleasure was knowing that even feeling the way he did Ally still turned up for me – crutches and all. He was simply delighted to get involved in the celebrations at last after missing out at the ground. We go back a long way together – to the days when he was a would-be sweeper and I was a shot-shy striker – but I was delighted he made it that night and we didn't have *too* quiet an evening.

Of course, the real celebrations were still to come when we made it three out of three with our Scottish Cup final victory. The previous season, when we won the double against Airdrie, I suffered an agonising race against time to be fit and take my place at Hampden. And after overcoming that, I found myself in the same position again as we prepared for the final hurdle at Parkhead. We had to face Aberdeen in a meaningless end-of-season clash at Pittodrie a few weeks before and lost 1–0, during which I picked up a back injury. I was terrified that having just made it the last time round, on this occasion I was going to miss out at the death. We were already missing Ally and Trevor Steven, which was a real blow for them, but once again, the two-week gap between the end of the League season and the final meant that I scraped into the side.

Without that I wouldn't have been there, simple as that. But I was, and what a day it turned out to be. Beating Airdrie the previous season was good, but that day beat it all. I was delighted for myself, but also for wee Durranty. When you watch a video of that season, you can see his face tripping him when we won the League, because he didn't come on. But the manager did him a turn there, whether he realised it at the time or not. The pitch at Broomfield was rock-hard and there was the chance of a physical game against Airdrie. But we won the game and the Gaffer kept him out of mischief. Imagine how he would have felt if he had played and been injured. The end result was that he was immense in the final and went on to set the seal on a season that had been a marvellous one for him.

The week before the game people were asking themselves if we had burnt ourselves out, but nothing could have been further from the truth. We were so confident, we couldn't wait to get out there. Nothing was going to stop us. Seeing a sea of European banners and red, white and blue in the Jungle, the traditional Celtic end, was great, and even though you can't beat Hampden for a Cup final the atmosphere that day was superb.

Young Neil Murray grabbed the opening goal and the second, from Mark Hateley, more or less wrapped things up. I can even claim to have scored in a Scottish Cup final as the Dons' goal took a deflection off me. But even though a strike from Lee Richardson put us under a bit of pressure, there was no way we were going to lose it as a team chasing another goal is always more likely to give something away. There were a lot of heroes, but my man-of-the-match award has to go to Ian Ferguson. I've watched the match twice since then and you simply couldn't beat his work-rate – defending and going forward.

Fergie doesn't get the credit he deserves sometimes, but the manager knows what he can do and so do his team-mates. When you were playing in defence and someone was running at you, you always knew that Fergie was tracking back and would get a tackle in sooner or later, which made our job a lot easier.

For myself and the other Scottish lads who were on the terraces when we won the last Treble in 1978, wrapping up the clean sweep meant more than words can say. My dad took me to see those teams and now he was in the stand proudly watching me achieving the same. It was magic right up until the moment I was selected for the random drug testing afterwards. It was a warm day, we had all run our guts out and it ended up taking me two and a half hours, gallons of water and several lagers, to give them what they wanted.

Mark Hateley, the Doc and I missed the team bus back to Ibrox and the subsequent celebrations on Paisley Road West as every Rangers pub in the area emptied to mob the bus as it passed. And when I got back to Govan I missed the first 20 minutes of the celebrations there because I was in the toilet!

Once it all started to sink in we realised that we'd turned over Aberdeen in all three competitions. And no matter how many times their management claimed that their lads would learn from the experience, there's no doubt defeat like that does have a negative effect on players. Second prizes, like winning, can be habit-forming. Fortunately, we were doing all the winning. Had Aberdeen won the Cup that day, they could have been given a real boost for the following season. But with the roles reversed, we had already struck a blow in the campaign to come.

That term we were to blow the chance of back-to-back Trebles, something that had *never* been done before, when we lost to Dundee United in the Scottish Cup final and our performances in general had slipped. But we're still up there with the other Treble-winning sides and with talk of the League Cup being scrapped in the seasons ahead, who knows, we could be the last team to win all three domestic trophies, though I'd rather see us go on and do it again in this season or in the near future. With guys like Gazza and Brian Laudrup moving to Ibrox since then we must stand a great chance of staging a repeat performance, hopefully sooner rather than later.

Chapter Two

Just Champion

Nothing can touch a packed Ibrox for atmosphere on European nights. But when Gary McAllister volleyed home a corner kick seconds into our Champions Cup first-leg tie with Leeds United the silence was deafening. It was the strangest feeling to be playing with a constant buzz and noise all round the stadium – followed by a sudden and total silence, because of the ban on away fans. But, fortunately for us, that particular horror show was re-run at Elland Road and then the starring roles went to Mark Hateley and Ally McCoist in one of the most dramatic matches I've ever been involved in.

Getting into the Champions League was the big prize and it was the first time since I had joined the club that we had a decent run in Europe, having already ditched our Scottish Cup hoodoo. We'd suffered against Red Star Belgrade and Sparta Prague in recent seasons, and although we always reckon we're going to do well in domestic competitions, we felt that it was time we made our mark on the Continent. To get to that level meant the club, who picked up nearly a quarter of a million pounds for every point, and the players would do well financially. But no matter how big the bonus, the main motivating factor was to get there and test ourselves against the best. That chance doesn't come along too often.

UEFA's decision to revamp the European Cup competition was a winner from the very start. The four-team mini-leagues with the group winners meeting in the finals was a big hit with players,

29

who couldn't wait for the chance to pit their wits against some of the game's biggest stars, and with the fans, who were early relishing a taste of some top-quality European football.

Having been so unlucky in one-off Euro clashes in recent seasons, we were confident of making our mark if we could beat Leeds United in the second round. And that was a *big* if. Leeds had gone through in controversial circumstances against Stuttgart and the Battle of Britain, as it was quickly tagged, was soon being hyped up.

We were quite happy to face Leeds rather than Stuttgart because it would be a British-style game and German sides, like Bayern Munich, had always made it difficult for us. The Gaffer went over to the Nou Camp stadium in Barcelona to see the replay and came back happy that it would be Leeds. Howard Wilkinson's men had done superbly well to capture their first English title in 18 years and had some quality players, including Scots stars like McAllister and Gordon Strachan and, of course, Eric Cantona. And their performance against Stuttgart in the first game saw them ranked up there with their all-conquering Seventies' side, even though they were a goal short of going through. However, once we knocked them out, suddenly the English press decided they were just an average team!

The first leg couldn't have got off to a worse start, but again sheer determination got us back on level terms, before we finished 2–1 winners, with a little help from Leeds goalie John Lukic who pushed a corner into his own net. We needed the win, but having conceded an away goal, going to Elland Road was a massive challenge for us. However, we went into it and came out of it with so much confidence.

After the match at Ibrox in the players' lounge we could see that they felt they had won the tie, with the possible exception of their Scottish contingent of Gary McAllister and Gordon Strachan, who maybe knew better. The fact is that we could and should have scored more against them at Ibrox and we always felt we had the players, Hateley and McCoist, to punish them if we got the breaks. We got the impression we had been written off and that got to us.

Archie Knox, as Manchester United's former assistant manager, used his English contacts to get cuttings from the newspapers down there which promptly found their way on to the dressing-room notice board and naturally fired us up even more.

The Gaffer told us we had nothing to fear. We knew they were weak defensively so we were very positive. That year, the manager's tactics were excellent. On the pitch we defended well – and any team that does that is in with a shout. We also had players of real quality up front and others, like Ian Durrant, who were capable of lightning breaks. So all he said to us in the dressing-room at Elland Road that night was: 'Go out and play the way you did at Ibrox.'

Fear didn't enter the equation, because there were no Rangers fans – travelling supporters being banned from both legs because of fears of crowd trouble. In that situation, which Leeds had already faced, and Celtic were to encounter at Ibrox more recently, the lack of support makes you even more determined to go out and prove yourselves. Our attitude was simply 'let's show 'em'.

I don't think Walter even needed to give us a team talk. The boys were all focused and each knew exactly what he had to do. Walter just needed to supply the organisation. We were channelling everything in the right direction and thought if we could get a quick goal, as Leeds had, then we'd see what they were made of.

Going down the tunnel, United's theme tune, *Eye of the Tiger* from the *Rocky* films, was blasting out. It was supposed to get the crowd going and intimidate the opposition, but instead I turned to see Durranty shadow-boxing with a huge grin on his face, loving every second. And if we'd had more time we could all have picked up some fancy footwork from him!

With just about every football fan in Britain glued to the telly that night, it was also the chance to put all those who ran down Scottish football in their place. I had to make a tackle on Cantona seconds into the match as he broke clear, but once Mark silenced the home fans with that fantastic long-range volley, the rest, as they say, is history. The boys got the goals, Andy Goram had the game of his life and even though we took a battering in the defence Andy's positioning and reflexes were simply fantastic.

It was certainly the Battle of Britain. After we scored a second goal, they hit back to make it 2–1 and they had four or five chances to level, but defensively we were well organised. With big strikers like Cantona and Chapman they had won an aerial battle against Stuttgart and were prone to pinging in more than the occasional high ball. So our main aim was to keep them outside the 18-yard box where we knew they didn't have the pace to run away from you. And we defended well at set pieces, again trying to make sure nothing loose dropped into the box. The manager's tactics proved to be spot on again.

For me it was great to be up against a player like Eric Cantona. Since his move to Manchester United, which was the equivalent of me joining Celtic, he's simply become an even better player because he has better players around him. Alex Ferguson has given him a freer role and even though at that time he had been in and out of the Leeds side, for Fergie to get him at that price was a real steal. He's a fabulous player and one we knew we would have to watch very closely. He's certainly not been without his troubles since, with just as many headlines on the front page as the back, but we didn't have any problems at all.

At that level you have a real respect for your opponents – you know they must have done something right to be playing for a club in the top 20 in Europe – and Eric gave us that respect. He's a temperamental guy but he pays a high price for his talent as people are always out to nail him. Afterwards he was one of the few Leeds stars to be found in their players' lounge. He's certainly not someone to hide on or off the park.

The players' lounge, strangely enough, wasn't exactly four-deep at the bar. Over in the corner I spotted Minder star, the actor Denis Waterman, whose face was tripping him. My dad couldn't make the match, so the first thing I did was phone him from the bar as I knew he would be doing cartwheels. Cantona was virtually the only Leeds star who turned up and to be fair to him I think he realised they had lost to a good team. I couldn't make out a great deal of what he was saying, but at least he was there to shake your hand and wish you all the best for the future games. That says a lot about him. A lot of people say a lot of bad things about him but I think his attitude that night was worth a lot. I've got a lot of time for Gordon Strachan and Gary McAllister, but they were both posted missing. I don't think they could face it, which I can understand.

After a few celebratory beers we jumped back on the bus with *Simply the Best* blasting out at full volume, were waved off by a few 'Leeds' fans, who had the correct scarves but the wrong accents, and partied all the way to Manchester where we were staying before catching the first shuttle in the morning.

Simply the Best is the top tune on our lucky cassette which is played on the team bus before every game. The lads will tell you they're not superstitious, but Jimmy Bell, our kitman and driver, has a lot to answer for if it doesn't get cranked up at some point. When you're on a run like we were you always stick to a routine.

When the dust had settled, we realised what it was all about and our season really took off on the back of our European run. Leeds? Well, from pipping Man United for the title the previous season, their season crashed round about them and they ended up near-bottom of the First Division.

We had something to look forward to for the next three months. We knew we were in with a shout of doing something in Europe and that gave us a tremendous lift. At Elland Road, one of the first in the dressing-room after the final whistle was Manchester United manager Alex Ferguson. There's a great rivalry between the two clubs down there, but the main reason for his huge grin and shaking hands with the lads was that he was chuffed that we had put across our message to the English as well. You would have thought it was his side that had done the business and Archie asked him: 'Have we ever been on a losing side here? Every time we visit Elland Road we get the right result.' Man United had a great record against their Lancashire rivals and this, plus the fact that Fergie's probably had the Scotland v England thing rammed down his throat since he went to Old Trafford, made it a great night for him too. I think any Scotsman down south would have wanted us to win – they're forever hearing just what a poor relation the Scottish game is.

That night Gary Stevens had arranged a night out in Manchester and it was one to remember. The Rastafarian doormen on the club in question must have seen a few wild nights over the years, but definitely nothing like this! We returned to the hotel to find the champagne still flowing and nearly a hundred Rangers fans who kept the bar open until five in the morning. My favourite memory is of Stuart McCall, who, being just as hyperactive off the pitch, didn't bother going to bed and was still swigging champagne at 7.30 a.m. The manager turned to him and said: 'Stuart, we're playing Celtic on Saturday, don't you think it's time to stop drinking?' 'No,' says the wee man, as he headed for the bus with the bubbly. 'Why don't we keep the party going till Friday and give them a chance?' Hysterics all round, and even though we managed a few more beers when we got back to Glasgow, we still won at Parkhead with Durranty grabbing the only goal.

Our attitude might seem a bit unprofessional to some, but the atmosphere within the squad at that time was great. We were all enjoying ourselves and even though I don't think the manager minded us enjoying our victories, what could he have said even if he had?

The Old Firm match underlined just how much the Euro bug had caught on with our fans as that season was probably the first ever where a result against Celtic wasn't the be all and end all. We were competing at a higher level and still riding high on that Leeds result, so even though they were still delighted to get a win, defeat would have been met with a shrug and the hope that we could do the business in Europe. Later on in the season, in the second Parkhead clash, the players were amazed by the sea of red, white and blue created by the huge European banners which the supporters clubs had flown all over Europe.

What people often forget about our campaign is that the very first hurdle we faced in the European Cup campaign was against Danish champs Lynghby. Against a team like that, the biggest problem can be complacency. Every year continental sides are written off by the Scottish press and fans. Even Red Star, who beat us two years before, weren't too highly fancied and they went on to win it! It's true that Danish football isn't of the same standard as Scotland, but most of their best players play abroad and their national side are former European Champions.

The manager had told us that Lynghby were a useful team, technically, and they showed that in the first leg at Ibrox when they knocked the ball out well and created a few chances. What they didn't have was a quality striker to put them away. But over the two legs they caused us a lot of problems, although getting a two-goal cushion thanks to Mark and Pieter was great.

Copenhagen was a home from home. The Parken Stadium was similar to Ibrox and there was a great turnout of our fans. We had an early shock when they hit the bar, but Durranty got on the end of a well-worked move to make sure we went through by winning home and away.

As the manager is fond of repeating, the dividing line between success and failure in Europe is very thin. In the Premier Division you might not be in top form, but you'll still grind out a result. In Europe one bit of slackness and you're out. And playing in Scotland also makes it harder to play at a higher level. There's no doubt even another British side like Leeds were playing in a tougher league every week. More than half of the teams in the English First Division, now the Premiership, will give you a hard game. Up here, you don't have that level of competition. You play each other four times for a start, which is bound to cause a reaction.

Personally, I wish there was more of a battle for the Premier title, but we've now won seven on the trot and even teams who have won the championship in the past, have proved to be less of a threat, although Aberdeen and Motherwell have both run us close in recent years. But clubs have had to rebuild stadia to meet the requirements of the Taylor Report and it will be another couple of seasons before some of them get the cashflow to allow them to spend as much as they would like on top stars again.

If we were playing in the English Premier League, things would be a lot tougher against clubs like Manchester United, Blackburn and Newcastle who can match our support and spending power. And that could only help us when we step into the European arena. I'd love to play in a British League. Satellite television coverage has widened the boundaries and I'd love to be playing in London or Manchester and also bringing big sides and big stars to Ibrox. It may happen, and if and when, there's no doubt our victory at Elland Road and the run which followed played a part in bringing it closer, because we showed that some Scottish teams *can* compete at that level.

We went into the draw as British champs, but knowing we still had everything to play for. We had missed AC Milan in the draw, but we knew that having also won the Champions Cup, Marseille would be our biggest danger. So it was back to Ibrox with expectations higher than ever . . . and yet another disastrous start. We looked more like chumps than champs as they played some good football on a very muddy, soft pitch. But generous helpings of blue grit were again on the menu when we went two goals down before fighting back for the draw.

Goughie had to go off at half-time and we brought in 'Elvis' Pressley at the back before going two down. But Gary McSwegan proved to be our supersub with a great header that had the capacity crowd roaring us on again. And when Mark Hateley became a muddy marvel with a diving header to equalise, our confidence soared and we felt that just another ten minutes could have seen us snatch a winner.

The place exploded when Mark dived in at the near post – the fans were just as relieved as us. Marseille gave us a footballing lesson but we taught them a thing or two about never giving up. Normally losing two goals at home in Europe would be a disaster due to the away goals factor in knock-out ties, but in a mini-league we felt we had a chance to prove ourselves over a number of games.

Next stop was Bochum, the German town CSKA Moscow had switched the tie to from Moscow because it was 40 degrees below there. I don't remember it being much warmer in Bochum which, having been rebuilt after taking a pasting from the Allies during the war, looked about as exciting as Paisley on a wet Monday. The stadium was another product of the concrete jungle school of architecture, though the Russkis did their best to liven things up with a band – the Red Army Ensemble.

We had our own Blue and White Brigade on tour and some brisk bargaining ensured that some of the bandsmen emerged for the half-time performance minus a peaked cap or two. I always wondered how they got on changing the Scottish fivers they had received for them when they got back to Russia.

None of the boys was complaining too much about Bochum. For us it was another hotel room and another big game. Business as usual. And we would much rather have played there than Moscow, having sampled some Eastern European hospitality in Kiev a few years previously. There turned out to be quite a good atmosphere and, although CSKA were a fair side and did threaten, we grabbed both points through a crucial Ian Ferguson strike, which was a massive boost to one and all.

But it was a different story against Club Brugge, the Belgian Champions. We could have kicked ourselves over there for losing a soft goal. Alexei Mikhailitchenko attempted to head clear a long throw-in, the ball came off his shoulder and dropped to Tomasz Dziubinski to rifle the ball home from the edge of the box and in off the base of the post. Alexei took most of the blame for his gaffe, but I felt I should have dominated in the box and cleared the danger earlier, so don't feel too bad, Chenks.

In the second half, they would have been happy to settle for a point and we gave them what can only be described in Govan terminology as 'a right doing'. But once again we managed to pull a draw out of the hat with Piet Huistra blasting in the equaliser. Unbelievably, Coisty, who was also in the vicinity, actually dummied the ball for Pieter to blast it past their keeper from 10 yards instead of having a go himself. To get a point out of the match and to produce a great second-half performance was another lift and teams were starting to fear us as a side who would never surrender. Stuart McCall ran himself into the ground that night and Neil Murray gave another exceptional and incredibly mature performance, even though it was his first taste of Europe.

We were now level with Marseille going into the break from European competition. We had three months of Premier Division and cup fixtures before getting another taste of the Euro magic. As I've said, our performances helped us in our domestic campaign. People were constantly talking about it and as far as we were concerned the next games couldn't come quickly enough. It felt like the quickest season ever. Games were coming thick and fast. If I was lucky I had just five free mid-weeks, but like everyone else, I loved every minute.

If there had been drama and controversy in the previous three matches, the next hurdle, Brugge at Ibrox, was to be even more unforgettable for two very different reasons – Big Nissy's remarkable goal and the crushing blow of losing Mark Hateley, who was sent off. With those two incidents still fresh in the minds of anyone who saw the game, what is often forgotten is that Ian Durrant scored another classic goal, which Mark set up before his untimely dismissal. A perfect pass and great first touch were followed by a low accurate shot. But the celebrations were short-lived as Hateley was given his marching orders not long after.

It was a harsh decision. Had the referee been British, he would have been unlucky to have been shown a *yellow* card. With two big lads like Mark and Lorenzo Staelens, you're always going to get a bit of argy-bargy and Mark was only pushing him away after another elbow in the back when the referee caught the tail end of the action and decided it was time to clean things up. It was harsh and heart-breaking, particularly with a crunch trip to Marseille on the cards, and especially coming just days before the 2–1 defeat at Parkhead. But we had to accept it and cope with it – on the night and in the final two matches.

Our pitch took a fair bit of criticism that season, but I don't think Nissy could have picked a firmer spot for his deflected shot to bounce and spin over Dany Verlinden's head. We were all delighted that Nissy got that goal, his last for the club, which is the one he'll always be remembered for. But people forget that he had given Rangers a lot of great service in just about every position over a number of years. The following week Scott had to retire injured during our clash with Celtic on 20 March 1993. Our 44-unbeaten-game run came to an end and sadly it was the end of the road for the big man as well. We were all gutted for Nissy and I'd like to wish him all the best for the future. In the previous season he was a mainstay at the back before picking up an injury which allowed me back into the side. If he had been injury-free he would have been our best player over his few seasons at Ibrox. And he was also an asset in the dressing-room where his general good humour and some of the sickest jokes I've ever heard kept everyone going.

Nissy was honest enough to admit his goal against Brugge was jammy and if we're honest we'd admit that, being down to ten men, we would have settled for a draw. Getting another two points set the seal on another great performance.

A lot of people no doubt thought, 'Lucky Rangers'. But you have to work hard for that kind of good fortune and we were hoping to be just as 'lucky' against Marseille. They were still unbeaten and our clash was being billed as the decider for our group.

Despite our results, we were still the underdogs and again we fancied our chances. There were a few flaws in their make-up. They were bewildered after our Ibrox opener. Their manager couldn't believe they had nearly thrown that game away as their undoubtedly superior skills were blunted by good old British fighting spirit. I will never forget before that clash being asked by a couple of journalists for my thoughts on playing against Marseille. I replied that Rudi Voller was just one of a number of quality players and I couldn't wait to test my skills against theirs. This brought a few sniggers from a couple of pressmen who obviously thought that I was kidding myself on that I was as skilful a player as someone like Voller, Germany's World Cup striker.

I didn't say anything at the time, but I was less than impressed. No matter what level you're at, playing against the best brings out the best. It's all a matter of playing to your own and the team's strengths. Skill alone doesn't always win matches. Yes, they were a great side and Voller and Alen Boksic, his striking partner, were a real handful. But we didn't give up. That was our strength and we did play to it. Over the campaign we did ourselves justice, especially by winning the Treble in the same season. So the journalists' reaction, which was fairly typical regarding Scottish teams' chances, doesn't need any more comment.

Our trip to Marseille was our cup final. All the wives and girlfriends flew out for the game. I was desperate for my dad to go, but he couldn't make it. Missing Big Mark was our first problem. He had done well against Basile Boli, the man who scored the winner for Marseille in the Champions Cup final, and at every level for England and in the French League during his time at Monaco. He felt he could do the same again and cause them major problems, so his loss was a great blow although we did have Ally McCoist back in the side.

There weren't a great deal of chances, but we played well on the night among the fanatical support in Velodrome. People thought we'd be terrified going there, but it was great. There was a real carnival atmosphere and I loved the 90 minutes. Something that comes back to haunt me, though, was the moment after Gary McSwegan came on as sub and tried a shot from a near-impossible angle. I was running in unmarked at the edge of the box and I always think what could have been if he had passed to me in a better position instead of shooting.

Again we were gutted to go behind as Marseille hit us on the break. But once again Durranty was our hero. I was in the penalty box when the ball flew over my head. As I turned it seemed to be in slow motion as Ian caught the ball on the volley to squeeze the equaliser into the corner of the net. That gave us a chance going into the final game against CSKA Moscow, but we all regretted not being able to grab the winner that would have made sure of a place in the final against AC Milan.

We were confident we could beat CSKA again, so it all came down to what Marseille could do against Bruges. But for once our luck failed us. We probably created more chances than in any other Champions League game, but we couldn't find the net. We did everything but score and the campaign came to an emotional end as the fans shed tears with us and gave us a standing ovation.

With Marseille doing the business in Brugge, it wouldn't have made any difference, but to have come so close, reaching the equivalent of the semi-final and remaining unbeaten, made me proud. We were a credit to ourselves, club and country. Even now, I don't think we fully appreciate just how much was achieved that season.

Goughie correctly pointed out in the aftermath, that the only way to top it was to win the European Cup and, as we were soon to discover, that was a tall order. There have only been five Treble-winning teams at Ibrox and we've found success in Europe just as hard to recapture. That's why you have to enjoy it while you can. You never know when the chance will come again. Personally I haven't played in European competition since, due to a combination of injuries and some early exits at the hands of Levski Sofia and AEK Athens. And with my new coaching role, that Moscow clash could well turn out to be my last at that level. But after European disappointments in my early years with the club the Champions League was a fantastic experience. A lot of the memories are on the pitch, but for the fans it was a terrific experience too. Talk about trains, planes and automobiles . . .

My favourite story is about the fan who turned up on the morning of the match at Glasgow airport, produced a passport and some readies and talked his way on to a spare seat on the players' wives flight. He turned up at home at four o'clock the following morning with a match programme, but minus the milk he'd nipped out for in the first place. Needless to say his wife still doesn't believe that's where he was all that time!

Of course, most of the bears endured days on a bus and Alan Duncan, a mate of mine, tells the story of the lad on his bus who moaned all the way back from France about getting home for some good Scottish grub. The first thing he did when the bus doors opened in Glasgow was dive into his local Chinese takeaway.

We had an even bigger laugh back in the Ibrox dressing-room when we heard about the banter on the plane home. Someone wanted to know why the flight back took longer and a player's mum, who'll remain nameless, explained that because it was dark it was harder for the pilot to see where he was going so he had to slow down . . . We were howling when we heard that one.

On a personal level I was disappointed my dad didn't get to make that trip, but I think he was nervous enough watching on TV. But my brother did watch us in Leeds and it's nice for both of us to have experienced that night.

The manager said afterwards: 'What you've achieved won't sink in for years.' He was right. It was a great achievement for the team but for individual players each success meant different things. Our English players love putting one over English teams, and for Mark to score at Elland Road, when he was being ignored by England boss Graham Taylor at the time, was also satisfying. Even though Ally's won the lot and broken just about every goalscoring record north of the border, he didn't enjoy the same level of success in his Sunderland days, so his Leeds strike was just as precious, proving to a lot of people down south that he could do the business at the highest level. Andy Goram buried the myths about Scottish goalies with his performance that night. For Stuart McCall, who had stood on the terracings at Elland Road as a kid, it was also special. Ian Durrant proved he was capable of turning it on at the highest level. And Scott Nisbet went out at the very top . . .

Chapter Three

Accie Days

When I met up with Alex Ferguson at Leeds, we'd both come a long way since our first brief encounter more than a decade before. Fergie had been boss at St Mirren when I was just another young hopeful with their boys club.

I had cartilage problems then and I was out for six months before my career had even begun. My first game back after that injury was against Eastercraigs Boys Club, a top Glasgow youth side – and I scored a hat-trick! Fergie was there to see it and asked John Thompson, our coach, if I would be interested in signing on with the Saints, only to be told that it was too late as I had joined Hamilton the previous night.

When you're travelling by public transport, Blantyre to Paisley was a fair distance, while Hamilton was five minutes on the bus. I had been training with the Buddies for over six months and nothing seemed to be happening although I thought that if I did well they might sign me. And as a few of my pals, like Alex Taylor and Paul Denholm and Robert Clark, who was an ex-Rangers S form, were playing with the Accies, when they showed an interest, there was no real contest.

Before we go any further, let's get one thing straight – I'm not from Stirling, in fact I've been there about twice. Just about every newspaper article over the years has referred to this 'Stirling-born' player, as a result of a mistake in one of the League books (it's actually Lennoxtown in Stirlingshire) which gives your date and place of birth, previous clubs etc. It has been repeated every year since. These days, home is Glasgow, but after early years in West Lothian, most of my growing up was done just off the Stonefield Road in Blantyre, about 15 miles outside the city in the industrial heart of what used to be the steel towns and coalfields of industrial Lanarkshire.

The biggest influence on my early days was undoubtedly my dad Andy who played in goal for a string of junior clubs. He turned out for St Anthony's, whose ground was just along the road from Ibrox, Bathgate, Pumpherston and had a year at Albion Rovers, although he didn't see eye to eye with their larger-than-life chairman Tom Fagan. As a kid I used to go and watch him regularly and I suppose my interest in the game, which was as strong as any Scots schoolboy's, was strengthened through that. I loved football and he helped push me on. Sometimes I didn't fancy playing, but he would always encourage me to get out there. My mum, Irene, was also keen on me sticking in at the game and both of them were a big help, particularly in those early days.

My older brother, David, was also a decent player when he was younger. If I'm honest he was probably better than I was, but he got injured and drifted away from the game. He could definitely have played at a higher level, but like so many others at a certain point he just stopped playing seriously. For everyone who makes it in football there are a dozen who could have been there too, but were distracted for various reasons and are happy to stay as amateurs, having a laugh and a few pints along the way. But personally, it was all I ever really wanted to do and I was prepared to make whatever sacrifices were needed to get there.

I was 12 when we moved through to Blantyre and soon after I had my first meeting with Ally McCoist. I scored against Ally's school when we drew 1–1 with them at Blantyre Vics ground in the East Kilbride Schools Cup. And then we went on to gub them 4–1 in a replay at Cambuslang. We all enjoyed the cup win at the time, but I didn't realise that it would still be something to slag off Coisty about 15 years later, though he claims the biggest factor was the crowd trouble in the first match!

My first manager at Hamilton was the former Celtic and Leeds player Eric Smith, but he was soon replaced by the former Celt Davie McParland when he went to join the ex-England and Leeds boss Don Revie in Saudi Arabia, coaching their national side. Eric was a crazy guy who loved his football. He used to run around in this massive Mercedes which doubled as a team bus. We turned up for a game one night and I swear about nine of us piled out when we got to the ground. His training methods were slightly unorthodox at times. He would have all the youngsters out on the park kicking the ball as high as they could into the air and then trap it with their bum. That's harder than it sounds, and painful, too, if you didn't get it right. You used to go home from training unable to sit down for the proverbial week.

Davie McParland, who had been assistant to Jock Stein at Parkhead in the late Seventies, was entirely different and I have to admit I wasn't too keen on him at that time. He was very knowledgeable about the game and these days I can appreciate a lot of things he used to try and drum into us. But at that age you tended to resent people telling you what to do and I thought he was getting at me, not trying to help.

After a brief spell in the youths and reserves, my professional career kicked-off when I made my League début against Clyde when I was 17. Every youngster dreams of playing for the big clubs, but it's just as much fun to star for your local side and I really enjoyed playing those first seasons in the First Division.

When Davie McParland left, John Blackley briefly stepped in before Bertie Auld became my third boss. Bertie was certainly a character and on his first day there, not realising every word in his office could be heard down in the dressing-room below, he was on the phone bemoaning the fact that he had 'not one player in this team'. The rest of the lads soon found out about it and set about trying to prove him wrong, although whether we did or not is a different story. But Bertie was just mad anyway, a real character.

John Lambie was next. We hit it off straightaway and I was soon captain. We got on well. He's a down-to-earth guy who likes dugs, pigeons and fitba', though not necessarily in that order. In man-management terms (though I'm sure that's a term John would never use!) he was the best. Players would run themselves into the ground for him.

John's just John and he's a brilliant guy, but you knew if you weren't doing what you were capable of on the park you would be in line for a real rollicking. His criticism was always constructive, though, and he'd point out where you had gone wrong. He was a total contrast to Bertie, who to me was still living on winning the European Cup with Celtic in 1967. I think he expected the standard of player he had to work with to be the same as the talented Celtic team he had played in, which obviously wasn't the case. You have to look at the level of the game you're involved in and he couldn't accept that, but John did and made the best of the resources he had.

There were always plenty of laughs at Douglas Park. During Bertie's days he used to wind us right up during team talks in the dressing-room, which wasn't the biggest, and where the players all squeezed in. One day Brian Wright, now Clydebank coach, put so much into his warm-up that he jumped a bit too high and smashed the light, plunging the place into darkness. Needless to say there wasn't a spare so we finished the team talk in candlelight.

Another not-so-funny dressing-room tale came when we played badly at Dumbarton one day. Roddy Hutchinson, who had played alongside guys like Andy Ritchie in the Morton side of the early Seventies, had a poor game and Bertie didn't miss him after the final whistle. 'What do you think you're up to with all those 60-yard balls to no one?' Bertie wanted to know. It got a bit heated before Roddy said sarcastically, 'Aye, you're a player, eh?' At this point, Bertie unbuttoned his shirt, and thrust his European Cup winner's medal, which was on a chain, into Roddy's face. 'Have you got one of them, son?' he asked. 'That's what it's all about.' It shut Roddy up, but it was a bit below the belt. Everyone knew he had played with a famous team, so there was no need to flaunt it.

Bertie was also the manager who, when he first arrived at the club, promised us that he believed in working with the ball at all times. 'Great,' we thought. 'No more lung-busting marathon runs.' Until the first day of training that was . . . when he told us all to put a ball under our arms and ordered us off on ten laps, keeping his promise about the ball work. 'You've got it under your arm, what more do you want?'

At Douglas Park, we used to pick up our wages on a Thursday night and head for Glasgow. If you walked out with 30 quid you were doing well, so we weren't exactly hitting the high-spots, but we had a laugh. One day we were in stitches before the game when one of the lads, George Daily, told us about his disastrous end to the Thursday session.

George, who stayed in Dumbarton, had blown his wages on a good few drinks and then merrily headed home only to be stopped on Great Western Road by a cop car.

'Do you know you've got a dodgy tail light?' was the first question.

'No,' says George, 'but I'll have it fixed tomorrow.' Bad move as the tell-tale whiff of alcohol has alerted the police to the fact that maybe he was not stone cold sober. After admitting to having 'a couple of beers' he was asked for his driving licence. 'I haven't got one.'

'What, with you?'

'Nope, I haven't got one at all,' confessed George.

This too is noted before, on discovering a distinct lack of road tax or insurance, the cops retire to put their heads together. The first one comes back across and asks incredulously, 'You've no licence, tax, insurance and you're well over the limit. Have you got *anything* to say?'

'Do you want to buy a car?' was the immortal line.

As you can probably tell, George was a priceless guy, probably related to Arfur Daly as it happens. He used to disappear for months on end and then turn up at training one night as if nothing had happened.

Playing for the Accies was great fun and on the park I picked up a lot of good habits, although I probably picked up a few bad ones off it from the older pros. From my point of view the good thing was that the boss was bringing in experienced players. Alex Forsyth, formerly of Rangers and Manchester United, Bobby

Graham, ex-Liverpool and Motherwell, former Celt Joe Craig and John Blackley were all guys whom you couldn't fail to learn from.

When we were warming up, Alex Forsyth would always be up at the front and he used to say, 'The day I'm not, means it's time to chuck it.' Other lads would complain that he was setting too quick a pace, but Alex was quick to point out that you train for your own benefit, nobody else's, and if you wanted to make it, do what you had to. That's something that's always stuck with me.

Another top-notch player with the Accies was Jamie Fairlie, who gave the club a good few years service. But he was unlucky enough to break his leg against Falkirk just when he was set for a move to Aberdeen, which then fell through. If he had gone there he would have been a real star. He was one of my favourites and I felt sorry for him when things turned out so badly.

I was really chuffed when one of my all-time heroes, Dave Smith, arrrived. Dave used to be able to ping deadly accurate 60-yard passes all through a game, which was fine if you were sprinting forward to get on the end of them. The big drawback was when he expected you to do the same during the warm-up or in training – you were knackered within five minutes!

The good thing about part-time football was that you had a good blend of kids who wanted to move on to better and bigger things and older players who were still enjoying their football, but had already played at the top level. Off the pitch there was plenty of learning to do from these guys as well. I was at a players' dance one night and the older boys slipped me a few drinks, so I was well on by the time a good-looking girl asked me to dance. I was chatting away to her in the course of the evening and she asked me how I was enjoying life at Douglas Park. 'It's great. I'm getting a few first team games and I'm loving every minute,' I told her. 'Apart from one thing. I hate that manager McParland of ours. He's a right b------!'

I went back over to join the lads at their table and as I sat down the first question was, 'What were you saying to her then?' before collapsing in fits as I told them. You've guessed it, it was the manager's daughter. She seemed a decent girl and I've got to thank her now for not saying anything to him or I would have been doing 20-minute runs on my own for weeks.

The old pros nearly got me into even deeper trouble on a Christmas night out when we headed for a Chinese restaurant in Glasgow near St Enoch bus station. I noticed groups of them heading away from the table and thought to myself that the toilets were in the other direction. But the penny finally dropped when the rest all piled towards the door, leaving me just a yard in front of an extremely upset chef with a meat cleaver in his hand. The guys were all part time, it wasn't like playing for a big club where we would be recognised, so they didn't really worry about this incident, though to me it was a fairly crazy experience.

Another character was a boy from East Kilbride, Jim Kean, who was a real Jack the lad. Whatever you wanted Jim could get it at a discount and he used to turn up to training on occasions with a suit rack so that the lads could get some cut-price clobber. Jim, who was a decent player, had been freed by Ayr before joining us, and as an act of revenge on his last day there he dived into the boot room on his way out and grabbed the first pair he could see. Unfortunately for him they belonged to the future Scotland and Liverpool star Stevie Nichol who is a size 12. 'The only guy at the club with flippers instead of boots,' moaned Jim.

On the pitch, another memorable moment came when George Best signed for Hibs and ensured that Douglas Park was sold out for the first time I could recall. The place was jam-packed and he didn't disappoint anyone. He had maybe seen better days, but what a player he still was. He did a couple of things in the first half that were pure genius, though, thankfully, the nutmeg he tried on me didn't succeed. It was a pleasure just to be on the same pitch.

My first full season started with a bang when I scored a hat-trick from full-back against Berwick Rangers and I'm proud to say that I'm still the only player in Scottish football to do that without the aid of a penalty, although at the time the boss shouted at me for being out of position so often.

John Lambie was eventually to sell me to Dundee for £45,000 after a fair bit of speculation that scouts for other clubs were interested. In the end I didn't go full-time professional until I was 22, probably because I had already had a few injury problems, including having both my cartilages removed by the time I was 15. But I'd always come back from injuries and played as well as ever. Far too many managers are far too careful with money. They should let the heart rule the head more often. Instead of going on about what injuries a player has had, they should find out what size his heart is and his attitude and aptitude for the game. If he loves the game, then take a chance. John Lambie always said, 'I don't really agree with medicals, if the guy has a big heart, I'll sign him.'

I think a lot of my problems when I was younger stemmed from the fact that we didn't have any facilities for building your body up, which are taken for granted now. If I had built up the muscle around the knees it might have supported them better, but all we ever did was train and play games, you never did any specialised training the way young lads at Ibrox work out in the multi-gym these days. No coach ever told me to do that. As far as they were concerned gyms were for weight lifters and boxers.

Towards the end of my final season, Accies had four games inside a week, including the reserve League Cup final against Dundee United at Tannadice, the final League game of the season against Clyde and in the Lanarkshire Cup. Six or seven of us played in every game, but we still managed to beat a strong United side with Davie Dodds and other first team regulars in it to win the reserve trophy. It was a nice way to finish my time there, having played a total of 133 first team games, and scoring 11 goals between my début in 1979 and 1984.

A few days later I was heading back to Tayside with John Lambie and our chairman, George Fulston, who is now with Falkirk, and we met up with Archie Knox. A deal was agreed within a few minutes and, although I think I ended up paying Dundee a signing-on fee to join them and Archie!

I was making decent money with my Accies wages and my full-time job as a time-served welder in Burnbank, just outside Glasgow. But there's no prizes for guessing which career I preferred. It was a dream come true to sign for Dundee and I was delighted at the chance to turn my back on that and play football for a living. I was delighted to get a crack in the Premier Division and turn full time at last.

Chapter Four

Opportunity Knox

On 3 May 1986 I became a Heart-breaker for the first time. Not in the pin-up sense, of course, but instead for helping Archie Knox's Dundee side rob the Jambos of the Premier Division title in the most dramatic fashion possible at Dens Park.

Under Alex MacDonald and Sandy Jardine, the Tynecastle team had strung together a fine unbeaten run which had all but clinched the League title and taken them to the final of the Scottish Cup. Now they just needed a draw or win to spark the celebrations their huge travelling support had travelled to Dundee for. Meanwhile, on the other side of the country, Celtic needed to beat St Mirren by at least four goals to pip Hearts at the final hurdle.

With just seven minutes to go, Robert Connor whipped in a corner kick, yours truly headed it on and Albert Kidd fired the ball past Henry Smith for his first League goal of the season. And two minutes from time he hammered another nail into their coffin with a second strike which cruelly snatched away the title from Hearts and reduced many of their fans to tears.

As the crowd spilled on to the park there was a mad scramble for the tunnel in the corner and I found my path blocked by a huge Jambo wrapped in maroon and white. My life flashed before me and a punch in the mouth looked like a sure bet until the guy dissolved in tears and just cried his eyes out as I quickly made my escape. Back in the dressing-room there were more shocks in store. We found our own chances of a European place for the first time in over a decade had been blown by Rangers who had done enough against Motherwell to clinch the remaining UEFA Cup spot. We also heard that Celtic had clinched the title with a bit of style, beating St Mirren 5–0.

In the end, of course, we helped Celtic's cause too, by mugging Hearts. However, what people often forget is that for us the chance of playing in Europe the following season was a big carrot. We were just as gutted to find out that Rangers had scraped through as the Hearts fans were at our result. Ironically, Albert's goals that day were his first League strikes of the season and it certainly ended Hearts' hopes. They lost 3–0 to Aberdeen the following week to end their Double-winning dream.

The following day, Robert Connor and I headed for Glasgow to play in Kenny Dalglish's testimonial match. And the first people we saw in the hotel foyer were Tommy Burns and Roy Aitken, who came over to shake hands and say thanks for helping them out. On the other hand Albert got a letter from some psycho Hearts fan saying, 'I'm coming up to Dundee to kill you . . . and tell that b------ John Brown he's next.'

When I moved from Hamilton, Archie signed Robert Connor for a similar fee around the same time, as well as guys like Stuart Rafferty, Derek McWilliams and Ray Stephen up front. We also had experienced guys like John McCormack and, latterly, Jim Duffy in the ranks, along with a young lad who's done quite well since, Blackburn Rovers' Colin Hendry. Jocky Scott, who was coach and took over from Archie, made nearly £700,000 from selling me and Robert a few years later. Archie had definitely been shrewd when it came to transfer business, although that was the one big disappointment at Dens Park, that every manager had to sell to survive.

I was more than happy to be there. I'd always wanted to play at the top level – it's the reason I started playing football in the first place. As I've said, injuries in my early years perhaps held me back as managers were scared to take a chance with my fitness. I had three and a half very happy years there and I relished getting the chance to pit myself against the best the Premier Division had to offer, including my old adversary from East Kilbride, McCoist.

Three of my most memorable occasions with Dundee came against Rangers, but for varying reasons. I always seemed to do well against the Ibrox men and on 16 February 1985 I helped dump them out of the Scottish Cup fourth round with a vital goal just nine minutes into the match. It was a great afternoon for Dundee and for me personally, but for Ally, who hadn't yet acquired the 'Super' tag, it was a day to be forgotten. It was just one of those afternoons that any striker has . . . the harder he tried the less chance he had of scoring. He never stopped running and was looking for every ball, but the ball just wouldn't go in. Eventually he bore the brunt of the fans' frustration and the chant 'Ally, Ally, get to f***' echoed round the ground. The punters just slaughtered him.

But Coisty was one of the few Rangers players who stuck out that afternoon. Most of the rest were posted missing and certainly weren't keen to get a hold of the ball and share any of the responsibility for the poor performances, as the game slipped away from them and the fans got on their backs. He was still there to miss the chances while other centre forwards would maybe have tried to hide and wouldn't have been in the box to miss them in the first place. He took terrible stick. I've never heard anything like it. Afterwards he was absolutely gutted and admits that he was in tears in the dressing-room. But as we headed for the tunnel I told him, 'Listen, you'll soon win the fans over, because you gave more than 100 per cent out there. And if you get as many chances as that in the future you'll score some amount of goals. Just keep your head up and you'll prove yourself in the long run.'

It might have sounded a fairly unrealistic assessment at the time, and I've no idea if my words of wisdom helped him or not, but nearly a decade, an MBE and two Golden Boots later, I think I can safely claim to have over 300 good examples to prove I was a better judge than the fans. He continued to give his all for the club. He could have let his head go down and moved on, but the fact that he stayed proved his love for the Gers.

Oh, and just to let you know, Ally, you weren't the only one who took pelters that night. After the game I was out with Alex

Forsyth, the ex-Ranger who also played with me at Hamilton, and our wives at a pub in High Blantyre called Carrigan's. They used to run a Rangers supporters bus from there and, predictably, it wasn't long before the bears were through from the bar and giving me dog's abuse for putting them out of the Cup. I was only out for a quiet drink after a meal, but I had to walk away from it and leave. I really couldn't believe it. They knew I was a Rangers man, but still gave me stick – and not for the last time either.

At that time we always seemed to have a wee edge on Rangers and my habit of scoring against them didn't make me too popular with my mates when I went back down to Blantyre. I used to take some stick from the Rangers punters, even the ones I knew and used to go to the Gers games with. They couldn't understand that I was a professional and you have to do what your team pays you for. When you go out on the park the only guys that matter are the ones wearing the same colour of jersey.

Another popular place for hurling abuse at me was Douglas Park. On my first visit there after signing for Dundee, I thought I would play it safe and try and gag Accies' legendary motormouth, Fergie. He's the fan who's been banned more times than anyone can remember over the years for the near-constant bad language and personal abuse he hurled at every visitor to the ground, and especially his own side. A few months ago he was allowed back into an Accies game at Firhill after a plea on medical grounds that he was suffering from depression because he couldn't watch his beloved Hamilton. Needless to say, he didn't even make it to half-time before being asked to leave. There was also the time he was getting a lift to a match on the team bus and was thrown out at a lay-by because he was destroying half the team's confidence before they even got to the game. It's a shame, because the guy is a real die-hard and loves the team, and there is far worse shouted by thousands of fans during your average Old Firm match or even on other terracings up and down the country. You don't see too many of them being thrown out, although Fergie's foghorn voice does make him instantly recognisable.

Having deserted the cause and gone to Dens, I was sure that I'd be a prime target in my first reappearance at Douglas Park, so I hatched a cunning plan to spare myself. As we stepped off the team bus, you could hear Fergie before you could see him, questioning parentage and family morals as usual. But he was silenced (briefly) when I pressed two complimentary tickets into his hand. 'Brilliant, Bomber, ta very much,' he said with a big grin, while I went off to get changed, happy in the knowledge that I was safe for the next 90 minutes.

I was wrong. He even wound us up before the game. As we were changing, his face appeared at a hole in the dressing-room wall where an air extraction fan had been. 'Duffy, ya baldy . . . ' was cut short as Jim hit him in the gob with a wet sponge. But it wasn't quiet for long. As we kicked off Fergie was right behind our goalie, Bobby Geddes, and he had him a bag of nerves for the entire match. I didn't care and I was still feeling quite pleased with myself when my tranquillity was shattered with: 'Haw, Broon, you're nothing but a useless, traitor, b------- . . . away and F-off back to Dundee!'

I was to finish top scorer at Dens Park in my first season in the Premier Division and I continued my Old Firm scoring exploits by finding the net against Celtic a month later in the quarter-final clash at Dens Park and again in May in the League at Parkhead. I had another good day against the Gers a few months later when I ensured my Trivial Pursuit status as the last man to score a hat-trick against them, including two goals in four minutes, on 23 November 1985, at Dens Park.

With 20 minutes gone, Tosh McKinlay was red-carded for a tackle on Ted McMinn and the old adage about it being more difficult to play against ten men was proved once again. When he trotted down the tunnel, the Dundee players looked at each other and gave a collective shrug of the shoulders. In a strange way it seemed to relax us and we decided to go out and enjoy ourselves.

The season had only just got underway; I had missed pre-season training and I hadn't shown any form at all. So what followed was even more of a surprise. For the first, I collected the ball just inside the Rangers half and set off on a run. I went past Davie McKinnon, bodyswerved another defender and angled a right-foot shot past Nicky Walker and into the corner of the net. Coisty went up the other end and equalised ten minutes later before we went ahead once more. We were awarded a free-kick. I hit it over the top of the wall and it curled from the keeper's right to the middle of the goals and in above his head. To be fair to Nicky, he might have been unsighted on that occasion, but he had no excuses for the third as there was no one else between us. Dougie Bell brought me down in the box and as I brushed myself off and set the ball on the spot Jim Duffy came running up to take the kick before I told him in no uncertain terms where to go. I was knackered by this point, but I just kept my head down and, knowing that Nicky usually picked a side to dive to, launched it right up the middle and into the roof of the net. Ally, who after that Cup nightmare had just as good a record against Dundee as I had against Rangers, grabbed his second shortly after that, but it was too little too late for them and we won 3–2.

Afterwards I was ecstatic and grabbed the match ball as a souvenir. I hung on to it even though Archie didn't want me to have it. He reckoned I was having a stinker of a season before that game and I didn't deserve it. The goals and the result meant a lot, especially with the score at nothing each when we were reduced to ten men. Robert Connor did well for us that afternoon and Jim Duffy was outstanding.

Archie had taken Dundee into the Premier Division and unlike a lot of newly promoted clubs we were enjoying a fair amount of success against our bigger rivals, especially in the Cup. We beat Rangers and met Celtic in the Scottish Cup and took them to a replay only to lose out. But having gone down to ten men after David Syme had, in our view, harshly red-carded Bobby Glennie, that was the difference between the teams. At full strength we were in with a shout, and who knows what could have happened if we had gone through then?

I didn't wear contact lenses at that time although Archie had been on at me for ages to get them. During that replay at Parkhead, we won a corner and even though it was all a blur for me, I thought I knew which direction the ball had taken. I was wrong. As I jumped at the near post the ball flew in and smacked me right on the nose before trickling out for a goal kick. I went to see about lenses the next day and even although it had been Archie's idea and one which would benefit Dundee's cause, I still ended up paying for them.

Apart from Old Firm clashes, we put together some great results in the Premier Division. Another match to remember was a seven-goal thriller in the derby match at Tannadice when I grabbed the winner, heading home a Rafferty corner to make it 4–3 and give us a rare victory over our neighbours.

In the three seasons I was there we were just pipped for a European spot by St Mirren and Rangers the following year. Even to be up there challenging was a major achievement for Dundee. But the biggest problem was that the club didn't have a great deal of money and with the bank on their back a lot of the time they were forced to sell their best players. Archie, of course, moved back to Aberdeen with Fergie and the two of them later headed south to take over at Manchester United.

In the close season when Archie left I was on holiday in Ibiza with Diana. I had vowed not to touch a drop for the whole summer and come back fit for pre-season, and even on holiday I stuck to my guns, trained twice a day and felt great.

Then one afternoon, a couple of Hearts fans who were at the same apartments broke the news that Archie was off to Pittodrie. 'Sod this,' I thought and jumped off the wagon in a big way. It was a mental evening and Diana eventually left me balancing on a plank of wood, drunk as a skunk, with the Hearts lads, whom I had got in cahoots with, trying everything to get me into the pool. Eventually they managed it and to my surprise, when I got back to the apartment, dripping all over the hallway, the door was locked. Women can be funny sometimes. It was all Archie's fault too.

I thoroughly enjoyed most of my time under Archie, but he could be a real b------ as well. One summer we went to Germany on a pre-season tour and not long into it Archie had to go home because of a family bereavement. A staff shortage meant Jocky, his assistant, had stayed at home with the reserves, so Archie was forced to leave the physio, Eric Ferguson, in charge, with the senior players taking training. To be fair to them, we did everything we should and worked hard . . . but we also went out on a bender for the three nights he was away. Even Eric was with us (bet you didn't know that, Archie), although he was trying to get us to take it easy. When the boss arrived back he called a team meeting and our hearts sank as we thought someone had blabbed. It was worse. 'I'm really pleased with the attitude you've shown and the work you put in while I was away, so I'm allowing you to have a night out tonight to go out and enjoy yourself.'

It was the last thing we needed, but we had to, otherwise he would have known for sure that something was far wrong with players wanting to stay in. It would have been unprecedented. We slunk out of the hotel foyer and after a couple of shandies we were back on top form again and another marathon session followed. This turned out to be an even worse idea as our considerate and fair-minded boss ran us into the ground the next morning and put us through sheer torture.

But that was Archie; he always liked to be fair with us. We were due to fly home after completing the fixtures on that tour when he told us that we'd been asked to play another game before we left. 'It's up to you, if you want to play or not. No one's forcing you, but we can get a later plane and fit it in if you want,' he told us. We were all desperate to go home by this stage, so our skipper, John McCormack, reported that the lads had taken a vote and decided to go home. 'Well, you're not! You'll play the game and that's all there is to it,' he raged. So much for player power.

On the same tour one of the games we played in Switzerland, at the foot of a mountain, was abandoned after half-time. The match started in 80 degrees of heat. But not long after, when a huge cloud came over the top of the mountain, a gale blew up and both keepers were struggling to kick the ball out of their area. I've never seen anything like it. The worst moment was probably when the beer tent blew away.

When Archie rejoined Alex Ferguson, Jocky Scott took over the hot seat and brought in some more fresh faces. Probably his most inspired move was creating the prolific striking partnership of Tommy Coyne and Keith Wright who scored a lot of goals for us. Before that I used to get forward and be involved in a lot of attacking moves, but when they arrived there was no real need. Keith supplied a lot of ammunition for Tommy to finish off. Tommy might have thought he had a rough ride across the street at Tannadice, but at that time they had a strong team and it was difficult to shift guys like Davie Dodds and Paul Sturrock from the attacking line. But once he got his chance at Dens, you could see what a quality player he was. I wasn't surprised that he went on to better things, including being capped for the Republic of Ireland.

Tommy and I have had our battles on the park since then, but I've always had a lot of time for him and it was a sad moment when I heard about the death of his wife, whom both Diana and myself knew from those Dundee days.

But he's fought back from that and is doing well for Motherwell, while Keith is happy playing with Hibs, the club he supported as a kid and, of course, he helped them dump us out of the League Cup a few seasons ago when they went on to win the trophy.

After their arrival, we enjoyed another bit of pre-season humour, this time at home in Dundee. There were 45 of us all set to start on a long run through the city's Camperdown Park when we heard gales of laughter from the back where the apprentices and YTS boys were. One of them had asked his mate, 'How long is a 40-minute run anyway?' We told him half an hour if he was quick. In the afternoon, after watching the Tour de France on telly over lunch at the ground, there was more mirth when hopefully not the same lad asked in all seriousness: 'See that Tour de France . . . is that in Switzerland?'

Dundee are in good hands now with Jim Duffy and John McCormack in charge, although, like their predecessors, they could still do with more money to spend. Their fans are crying out for a sucessful team and if they were to get back into the Premier and do well, their fan base would probably see them attracting more supporters than United.

John McCormack used to keep everyone going when I played beside him and like me he's had more than his fair share of injuries and more comebacks than Frank Sinatra. I remember the time he was so desperate to play and his knees were so bad he took some painkillers that were meant for his dog. I always knew he was barking mad but when he cocked a leg at the near post, it proved it. John's a walking wreck, but even though he was in a lot of pain he never complained and it's a testament to his determination that he managed to extend his playing career for so long.

Although most of my time at Dens was memorable, towards the end things turned a bit sour. I didn't always see eye to eye with Jocky Scott, and I was missing from the team list on a few occasions as I hit a bad patch of form that coincided with a period of discontent. But then, without any warning, things were to change dramatically and my career took another leap forward.

Chapter Five

Not a Billy Bhoy

It may be hard for those who know my Bluenose background to believe, but the man responsible for getting me my dream move to Ibrox was none other than ex-Celtic manager Billy McNeill! The occasion was a Sunday benefit match for Dundee's Jim Duffy at Dens Park against a Premier League Select on 6 December 1987, with Billy in charge of the League side. We won 5–3 and I grabbed another goal. Afterwards Celtic skipper Roy Aitken came up to me and said, 'Big Billy would like a word.' It was several actually and you could have knocked me down with a feather: 'I'm keen to sign you. I think you could do a job for us,' he said. 'But don't say anything to anyone or do anything. Just leave it to me.'

'Okay,' I said, before handing in a transfer request the very next day. My thinking behind moving so fast was that if he was interested, maybe some other clubs would be too. At that time I was going through a bad patch at Dens. I was in and out of the team, nothing much was going right and I would have jumped at the chance to move on. But after the initial approach I heard absolutely nothing more and by January 1988 it was too late for Billy to follow up – I was off to Ibrox. If I hadn't made myself available by asking for a transfer then Graeme Souness might have assumed I was happy where I was and never made an offer.

Around the same time I bumped into Tommy Burns at a players' do and mentioned to him that McNeill had expressed an interest in bringing me to Parkhead. Tommy just smiled, shook his head and said: 'Forget it.' Apparently it was Billy's style to tap a dozen players, keep his options open and probably never follow most of them up. No doubt there are other players who've been in the same boat and ended up very disappointed. But that was just Billy's way of operating. It worked out for me slapping in a transfer request, but there must have been others who had done the same and lived to regret it. And now, of course, I'm very grateful that he didn't pursue me, after helping prompt a move and put me in the shop window.

Would I have signed for Celtic? A million-dollar question. My heart would probably have ruled my head and as a Gers fan I would have taken a move down south first. But what if no one else had come in? At the end of the day you're a professional, football's your job and you have to keep your family, so who knows . . . Kenny Dalglish was a big Rangers fan and he managed it, but Kenny was something special and I think with the Parkhead punters well aware of my allegiances, it might not have been a good move on Billy's part either. And anyway, it would have meant that I would have missed out on the chance to score against the Celts at Parkhead on Ne'erday, which is a very special memory!

While all this was going on I caused a bit of a furore in the Morton dugout and the Dundee team bus during a trip to Greenock. I hadn't been in the side and the manager had brought me back unexpectedly for the match, so I'd been out for a curry and a few beers the night before. With ten minutes to go, at 7–1 up, I was dying to go to the toilet, but with both our subs used I had to leave us short in numbers before I was caught short. When I went into the dressing-room, the guys in the bath thought at first I'd been red-carded, but a few minutes later I trotted happily back on to the pitch – with some toilet roll hanging from the back of my shorts. It was meant as a joke, but, unfortunately, Morton boss Allan McGraw didn't see it that way and was about to blow a gasket. Looking back, it was maybe a bit disrespectful, but it wasn't really intended that way and it was funny at the time.

He wasn't the only one who was upset. Dundee chairman Angus Cook had spotted Billy McNeill and Walter Smith in the stand and when I went off the field they disappeared too – probably

Ally over . . . the goal that dumped Rangers out of the Scottish Cup in February 1985, and led to Coisty taking flak from the fans. (*Sunday Mirror*)

The equaliser . . . another Old Firm cracker against Celtic. (*Fotopress*)

Derby delight . . . after scoring the winner for Dundee against United at Tannadice, with team mates McWilliams and Harris and United's Dodds, Malpas, Thomson and Narey looking on. (*Fotopress*)

Cup that . . . Mark Walters, me, Neale Cooper, Ally McCoist and Kevin Drinkell celebrate at the end of the 1988 Skol Cup final after a 3–2 win.

On yer bike . . . hard at work at Lilleshall. (*D.C. Thomson*)

Italian job . . . for Mo Johnston after his controversial signing in July 1989 as we take a well-earned rest at our Il Ciocco training camp. (*The Sun*)

The way we were . . . the Light Blues line-up in Italy in July 1989.
(*Mike Schofield/Rangers News*)

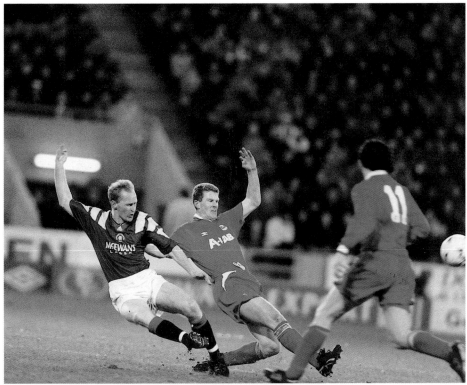
Don for . . . battling with Aberdeen's Duncan Shearer at Pittodrie.
(*Rangers News*)

Time out . . . a quick word with the referee during our Champions League clash
with Marseille at Ibrox. (*Rangers News*)

Blue heaven . . . on a lap of honour at an Ibrox championship-winning party.
(*Rangers News*)

Ripping yarns . . . having a tear-iffic time at Ibrox. (*Rangers News*)

Eyes down . . . on the attack with Oleg Kuznetsov trying to stop me during a
pre–season friendly. (*Daily Record*)

assuming I had an injury and wouldn't be back out. On the team bus, wee Angus was fuming and accused me of being tapped, which I could only deny, but he wasn't convinced and nothing I could say would make him change his mind. Angus, if you're reading this, you were right!

Around the New Year period in season 1987–88 we faced Rangers twice within the space of a couple of weeks. In the first match we lost 2–0 at Ibrox and in the second the score was 1–0 in their favour at Dens. Two of the goals were carbon copies of each other with Ian Durrant crossing the ball and finding McCoist, who by then was enjoying a lot more goalscoring success, especially against Dundee.

In the second match, we came into things a bit more and I pushed forward into midfield . . . and nearly ended my Rangers career before it had begun. Graeme Souness and I clashed in the centre of the park after a tackle from me which had no chance of winning the ball, but certainly got his attention and the referee's as he produced the yellow card. As I stood over him I was surrounded by an angry mob including Terry Butcher, Graeme Roberts and even Coisty, obviously upset at the treatment I had just dished out to their player/manager.

We were getting beat, I was frustrated and decided it was time to put my point across. Things were looking nasty, although I'm sure I could have looked after myself, until Souness looked up and told them to leave me alone.

In a previous match Graeme had caught me with a dig in the kidneys that left me unable to move for ten minutes. But there were no hard feelings. I put it down to experience and when I crunched him the next time round he could accept it. He liked to dish it out when necessary, but he could also take it and shrug it off. Still growling, they backed off and he got back on his feet without another word. The next time I spoke to him it was me who was floored when he asked me to sign for Rangers.

Chapter Six

Blue Heaven

The day after that eventful clash with Rangers and Souness, the phone rang in our house in Carnoustie. Diana told me it was 'Graeme' and like me assumed it was a local pressman who was a regular caller.

I couldn't believe it when I heard the distinctive tones of the Rangers boss. My first thoughts were that after the previous day's performance someone was on a major wind-up and it took me a few seconds to realise it was a genuine call. He came straight to the point. 'Would you be interested in coming to Ibrox?' were about the only bits of the conversation I could remember. And, of course, there are no prizes for guessing the right answer.

The Gers were up against Steau Bucharest in the Champions Cup, having recaptured the League title at Pittodrie during Souness's first season in charge in 1986–87. If they beat Steau and went further in the competition and I signed right away I would be in the frame for the next round. But that meant telling Dundee that I wasn't fit to play in the local derby against United that Saturday. At the time, Dundee had a seven-point lead over United and were going for a place in Europe, so it was an even more important fixture than usual. They wanted me to play, but Graeme was on the phone about three times a day.

'I heard other clubs are interested in you,' he said.

'I'm not interested in other clubs,' I replied, which I think he liked because it showed I was committed to signing.

'We'll still sign you if you play against Dundee United, but if you do, you'll miss the European deadline,' he continued.

The next day I told Jocky Scott that I was struggling for the Saturday and he told me to see the physio Eric Ferguson. I did and repeated the same line and made it clear I wasn't available. I had made up my mind that was it. Either sell me now or I'm not playing on Saturday anyway. In the end, even though I was to sign on the day of the UEFA deadline, it wouldn't have mattered as Rangers lost out to Steau.

I still don't feel bad about that decision. And it wouldn't really have made any difference had it been Archie Knox, who in general I had had a better relationship with than Jocky. Archie gave me some rough treatment in my early days at Dens too. My mind was set and I thought 'I can't miss this opportunity, especially after the Hearts debacle. It's time to look after number one'. After 131 games in a dark blue jersey and scoring 36 goals in my three and a half years there, it was time to move on.

When it happened, Jocky crucified me in the press, pointing out that I had signed a new contract shortly before and questioning my loyalty to the club. Fair enough, I took a bit of flak, but I didn't let the team down on the park – ever. If you ask the fans, whom I always had a good rapport with, they'll tell you that when I was asked to play I never gave less than 110 per cent. No one could criticise me for that. And although managers are well paid to trot out that kind of line, as it's their job to represent the club and do their best for them, it only seems to apply until they jump ship themselves. Contracts seem to apply to everyone except them, which is bit hypocritical.

When that call came I had made up my mind and for me, Diana, and my mum and dad and the rest of the family, it was the longest week ever. On the Thursday, Jocky phoned and said: 'We've accepted a bid for you, you can drive down today.'

'Fine, where to?' I asked.

'Don't kid me on,' he snapped. It carried on like this for a while as I insisted I hadn't a clue what he was talking about until finally he said: 'It's Rangers, as if you didn't know, and you can go down straightaway.'

I jumped in the car and headed for Glasgow at top speed and I can't remember a thing about the drive down.

At Ibrox I was given a medical and after the Hearts fiasco when I failed this particular hurdle, my blood pressure must have been sky high. Jan Bartram was there too and I asked the Doc if Hearts had any justification for knocking me back on physical grounds. 'No, the injuries you've had, everyone knows about and the effects can be clearly seen. There's still nothing to stop you playing,' he said, adding that if they had used that as an excuse, it was likely that there was some other reason for their U-turn. Thankfully everything went well and I headed back into the treatment room.

Graeme arrived with a piece of paper with a figure written on it and I agreed. That was it. No negotiations, no agents, just where do I sign and it was done, with my arrival taking Souness's spending over the £5 million mark. I headed home that night with an understandably huge grin on my face and then back down the next morning, feeling like a kid on Christmas day.

One of the first people on the phone that night was Archie Knox, whom I hadn't spoken to for a few years. He called from Old Trafford to wish me all the best. It's small things like that that you remember and appreciate.

On the Friday night we stayed at Di's mum and dad's, before I was scheduled to make my début against Hearts at Tynecastle. It was only then that it all sunk in. I was in the room myself and I don't mind admitting that the tears flowed. A lot of it stemmed from the let-down with Hearts which had left a nasty taste in my mouth and upset all of my family. After that I was wary of the same thing happening again – it's not exactly unknown for transfers to be called off at the last minute. So it was an emotional time, but once that was over it was a matter of getting on with the playing side and, like me, my family were overjoyed. It meant a lot to them that I had finally made my dream move.

My first day in the dressing-room was great. I'd known Coisty for years and a few of the other lads, but just to be in the same dressing-room as boys like Chris Woods, Terry Butcher, Graham Roberts, Goughie and Ray Wilkins was like a dream. I was flying.

It was the best feeling in the world and I wasn't to know it, but from there on there were to be even more highs, though not until the following season.

I made my first appearance at Ibrox in a Rangers jersey in front of 41,000 against Falkirk along with £180,000 signing from Silkeborg, Jan Bartam, with both of us making scoring débuts. I must have lost half a stone beforehand through worry. I didn't sleep a wink the night before and I was so desparate to do well I ended up trying too hard. At half time Souness told me to calm down, start stroking the ball around and things would happen for me. It worked. My play improved and shortly after I saw off a challenge from the Bairns' Ian MacLeod and banged in my first goal for the Light Blues. Having been signed as a midfielder, I also made my first appearance in the Rangers defence that day when I moved back to fill the gap left by Graham Roberts's early departure with an injury.

One of the things I had to get used to quickly after signing for Rangers was being recognised in the street. This can be a nice experience, especially if it's by your own fans. The day I arrived at Ibrox, I was heading out of the front door when this old woman stopped me and asked for my autograph for her grandchildren. 'I'm sorry to bother you son, I'm sure you must get a lot of this,' she said.

'Not at all,' I insisted, not wanting to tell her that she was the first person to ask for my autograph as a Rangers player.

A few months later, still not having adjusted to the realities of my new-found fame, I was heading off to meet Coisty at a pub in Old Kilpatrick near Clydebank to watch an international match when I was recognised again. I hadn't long moved to Glasgow so I decided my best bet was to jump on the train, not realising that it was about four p.m. and there was a secondary school nearby. As I walked along the platform, half a dozen teenage boys spotted me. The wee gallus one among them said: 'Are you John Brown?'

'No, son, I'm not,' I replied and walked on.

I could hear them arguing amongst themselves and the wee guy approached for a second time and asked me again. Their debate continued with the other lads taking the mickey out of him for getting it wrong. 'Right, I bet you a pound,' he said and came over again.

'Look, mister, I've just bet my mates, it is you, isn't it? You *are* John Brown.'

'No, sorry,' I told him.

'Well, you're just as ugly as the big b------,' was his parting shot.

The one place I hadn't been shown round at Ibrox was the Trophy Room and it was to be nine months before I finally gave myself an unguided tour, having decided that I wouldn't set foot in the door until I had helped to bring a piece of silverware there.

Even though I was moving to what would be a vastly successful Rangers outfit, that season there were a few disappointments in store. After capturing the long-awaited League title at Pittodrie, we failed to make it two in a row, losing in the title race to Celtic's double-winning side. But, even after all the upheaval of Souness's arrival in 1986, the front door at Ibrox should have been a revolving one as the transfer wheeling and dealing continued. I signed on the same day as Jan Bartram, the Danish full-back, and the Gers had already brought Richard Gough on board from Spurs and Mark Walters from Aston Villa. There were so many changes in personnel it was obvious that it was going to take a while for the team to gel together and our cause wasn't helped by Terry Butcher, who had been inspirational since his move north, struggling for form and fitness after breaking his leg. Chris Woods was also hit by injury. The manager was obviously hoping that we would get through it, even with so many new faces, but it just wasn't to be.

In the previous season, the title win at Pittodrie was unexpected as it was Walter and Graeme's first season in charge. But the following year they found it tougher going. That failure is even more significant now when you consider that a victory could have brought the Blues even closer to Celtic's record of nine-in-a-row League championship wins!

Personally, my worst moment in the first season was being sent off in a crucial Scottish Cup fourth round tie against Dunfermline which we went on to lose 2–0 after I'd been been given my marching orders in the first half. It was the first (and last) time I'd ever been sent off at first team level and the memory of it today still makes me mad. It was a simple clash of heads with the Pars winger Mark Smith. I stepped out as a cross ball came in and he stepped back. Simple as that. Even the player came out afterwards and said it was a pure accident, but that didn't stop the referee from bringing out the red card and Ray Wilkins having to hold me back as I questioned the official's view of things.

I reckon that Dunfermline manager Jim Leishman's antics on the sidelines didn't help and the ref, Alan Ferguson, who retired that year and later told all in his memoirs, claims that his linesman told him I had pushed the player to the ground and should be sent off – which wasn't the case. He denied that Leishman or the Dunfermline players' ranting and raving had anything to do with the decision and he had also changed his story. When I spoke to him about his decision that afternoon he claimed that his linesman had spotted 'a vicious blow with an elbow', which wasn't what he said in the press later on. Television commentator Gerry McNee got in on the act by agreeing with the linesman. When I asked him about this later he said he had caught it out of the side of his eye. Now how you can 'see' that from the stand when you're not focused on it I'll never know.

I was raging with the ref who always struck me as the type who was more interested in being centre stage than the players. You wondered sometimes with the amount of aftershave he used to wear on the pitch whether he was dressed for football or ready for a night on the town. He always wanted to be noticed, and I think the best referees, like Brian McGinlay, are the ones you don't see on the pitch and who can do their job without getting in the way.

That little affair also cost me my Old Firm début, which was maybe just as well as we lost 2–1 with Jan Bartram getting our goal. Looking back, that was probably the start of a trend. Since then I've missed just about the whole of March in every season, either through injury or suspension as the totting up of disciplinary points meant an automatic ban. Souness was quick to point out that 'I need players on the park, not in the stand', and since then my record has been pretty good. A lot of people who perhaps consider me as a tough player might be surprised to find out that was my one and only red card in over a decade of professional football, and although I've picked up the same number of yellow cards as defenders expect to, I think my record speaks for itself.

Another début I missed that term was in Europe. Even though I had signed in time to meet the deadline for the next round in the European Cup, we didn't get there, thanks to Steau Bucharest, though I must admit I enjoyed the night they came to Ibrox – but not because of any of the on-field action. Mark Walters had signed a month before I had and he had been on at me and a few other lads about learning some Rangers songs to sing at supporters club functions. That night, the atmosphere against Steau was tremendous and at one point the entire stadium launched into a chorus of 'Hello, Hello we are . . .' Mark, who like myself and Jan Bartram, wasn't eligible for the match, turned to me and asked, 'What's that they're singing?'

I refused to tell him and said, 'What do you think they're singing?'

Two seconds later he'd worked it out and launched into 'Hi-ho, Hi-ho, we are the Billy boys' in a thick Brummie accent.

For me it wasn't a laughing matter that we failed to clinch the title that season as Celtic swept to the Double in their centenary year. In the end it took me until the following season, in October 1988, just days after the infamous tackle on Ian Durrant at Pittodrie, to win my first medal at Ibrox.

It was harsh reminder to see Neil Simpson playing that afternoon while Durranty was on crutches, but there was never any question of it being a grudge match or turning nasty. Instead, the fans were treated to another entertaining final: one that perhaps didn't hit the heights of the previous season's dramatic victory, which had been hailed as a classic, but which was still a five-goal thriller with a nail-biting ending.

Who else but Coisty could have grabbed the winner with just a few minutes on the clock after earlier goals from himself and Ian

Ferguson had been cancelled out by a double from Davie Dodds? Doddsy, who loves to wind everyone up by claiming that he's the Premier Division's all-time top scorer if you take away McCoist's penalties, also never tires of reminding us that he was given the man of the match award that day. The lads usually get their own back by reminding him that they have a winner's medal and a win bonus which helped go towards redecorating their house – not a couple of cans of lager and a loser's medal.

That night back at Ibrox, I was finally able to get my first tour of the Trophy Room. Diana had a tear in her eye and I wasn't far away from crying myself. After nine months at the club, I finally had a winner's medal and I felt as if I had arrived at last . . .

Chapter Seven

Hearts Attack

The goal I scored to put Hearts out in the Scottish Cup quarter-final at Ibrox in March 1994 was a special one. Scoring at Ibrox, especially to clinch a place in a semi-final, is always different class, but that one meant even more as it gave me some revenge over Hearts for a transfer debacle I was involved in seven years previously.

Not that I've got anything against the club or their fans, both of which I rate very highly. My bad memories can be summed up in two words – Wallace Mercer. He was in control of the club when they put me through a shattering experience which at the time cast a shadow over my entire career.

A few months after I had helped end their title dream at Dens, we were up in the Highlands on tour when rumours of their interest in signing me started to circulate. I played in a few games, scored a few goals and went back to Dundee where Jocky Scott told me that they had accepted a bid and I was go and speak to Hearts the next day. I was enjoying my football at Dundee at that point and I wasn't desperate to go, but they weren't the type of club who would offer you a better deal to stay. They were quite happy to move someone on to keep the bank manager happy.

I drove down the next morning and was greeted at Tynecastle by the co-management team of Sandy Jardine and Alex MacDonald. After some discussion, I showed them a bit of paper with a figure on it and they unanimously decided that Wallace Mercer wouldn't be likely to be offering anything close, either in a signing-on fee or on wages. Alex and Sandy were decent enough and I was looking forward to working under two guys who were heroes of mine when I was younger, but they took a back seat when it came to financial dealings, so my next meeting was with Mercer himself.

His co-managers turned out to be right. 'Oh, no,' he said, shaking his head as he glanced at the same piece of paper, ' . . . and you want that tax-free?' I told him that's what it would take for me to move and after another five minutes he suggested I go and get a medical and said, 'We'll come to some agreement.' I didn't think there was much point to all this if we weren't going to come to terms. Agreement didn't look likely at that stage, but Wallace then insisted on giving me a guided tour of Tynecastle, proudly pointing out various improvements, though all the while I just wanted to get on with the business in hand.

Eventually we sat down and after a bit of give and take on both sides came to agreement on a contract. I then headed off with the team doctor to be checked out by a specialist at the hospital before completing the deal. After the medical I sat outside while the doctor discussed it with his colleague, then on the road back to Gorgie we chatted away and he asked me where I fancied staying in Edinburgh, advising me to make it outside the city because it was cheaper and so on.

At this point I assumed everything had gone well and it was just a case of signing on the dotted line. So when I walked back into a room that contained our chairman Ian Gellatly, Mercer and Pilmar Smith, the Hearts vice-chairman, it was like a slap across the face when I was told: 'I'm sorry, the deal's off . . . we've had problems with your medical and we feel signing you is too much of a risk.'

Our chairman was looking less than happy and Sandy Jardine came over and said: 'I'm sorry, John. I know how you feel.'

'No, I don't think you do – you were never rejected like this during your career,' I replied. And that was it. There were no further discussions and I was left high and dry.

Anger came later. At that moment I was just devastated.

Sandy walked out to the car with me and I drove round the

corner from the ground and sat for five minutes to compose myself, otherwise I would probably have crashed on the way home, I was so wound up.

When I got into the house, Diana was there with a friend. I walked past them and into the bedroom without saying a word. She followed me, knowing that something had gone wrong and when I told her she burst into tears. Like me, she had been excited at the prospect of a move and when it collapsed around us it had a shattering effect on both of us and hurt a lot of people close to me. I felt just like a piece of meat. And that kind of situation makes you realise that for all the money professional players can earn in the game, the real power and the decisions that affect their lives every day of the week are in someone else's hands and they're just there to be used and abused as pawns in someone else's game.

After that fiasco I felt as if there was no chance of me ever getting another move. I was now branded as a crock. Hearts stated that the deal was off because of a failure to agree personal terms, but it didn't take the news long to leak out and that bothered me a lot. Needless to say it took me a while to get my career back on track and I felt as if Mercer had dumped on me from a great height.

Perhaps they didn't have a great deal of cash and had to spend wisely, but as I've already said, none of my earlier ops and injuries were a big secret and when I think back to my conversation with their club doctor, he seemed quite happy with the results of my medical. I had had normal problems with hamstrings, calf muscles and niggly strains, but since my last op at 21 during my Hamilton days, I had had no problems at all and I'm sure Hearts knew all this before they made an approach, so it still puzzles me why it should have been a factor later on. Dundee knew all about that and, even though the cash involved was less, they didn't see me as a risk, and neither, eventually, did Rangers – they wound up paying nearly £150,000 more than Hearts.

I still don't think my fitness was the real issue. Perhaps Wallace had second thoughts about the deal we had struck and had figured on getting me to sign for less. No matter what, the way he had treated me was shabby.

It's a few years ago now, but forgiving and forgetting isn't one of my strong points. That's always given me a bit of extra dig against the Jam Tarts and when I scored against them in that Scottish Cup quarter-final match, I had my first real opportunity to have a word with the press on the subject and thanked Wallace for giving me the chance to sign for the club I had always wanted to. If I had gone to Tynecastle, I'd probably still be there now and never have made the move to Ibrox.

I hadn't gone over the top in my comments, but a fax arrived at Ibrox the next day demanding an apology for my conduct. I think the headline 'Super Wally' was what upset him the most, but then I don't write the headlines, although I thought it fairly apt after what had gone before. In his message, Mercer said he was 'devastated' after agreeing terms to be 'advised and instructed by my club doctor and vice-chairman that we could not conclude the signing. That decision was taken for me . . . '

Now, I think even Wallace would be the first to admit that when he was in charge at Tynecastle he was pretty much his own man. He might have taken some advice now and again, but being the major shareholder no one could 'instruct' him to do anything. So to blame others for the decision doesn't ring true and I think he should be man enough to accept the responsibility.

And I still don't accept, having being given the all-clear by the medical team at Ibrox, that the Hearts club doctor, after the conversation we had about moving to Edinburgh, was anything but happy with the medical results. Wallace went on to say that the headline and other reports 'just increases the pain and anguish not only felt by myself and my family, but within my own club by our senior professionals . . .' Putting it mildly, I don't think his feelings over a headline even came close to what myself and my family felt after being let down so badly in 1986. After a while it didn't bother me so much, but for what he put my family through there's still no love lost between us.

The Gaffer asked me to respond and eventually I did. But I don't think it was the apology Wallace was expecting as I pointed out that I was sorry that he felt that way, but not for what I had said, and pointed out that my words and the headline didn't really tally, so I couldn't be held responsible for that.

I still have a great respect for Sandy Jardine and Alex MacDonald. At the time they had built up a side that could challenge for honours and I thought it would be great to go there, especially to a side with such loyal backing. And I still can't understand the reasons behind it. I don't know whether after our haggling Wallace was comfortable with the money involved and whether it was in his budget or not, but it was the same basic wage with a bigger signing-on fee which shouldn't have posed a problem. If it had been the cash, it would have been more honest to come out and say it, but maybe he didn't want to admit that even those kinds of sums weren't practical for them.

Only Wallace knows why he made a U-turn and I don't expect I'll ever find out the truth behind it.

As I've said, I bear the Hearts players and fans no grudge, but on a later occasion I found myself involved in even more controversy with the club. During a match at Ibrox, not long after Mo Johnston had signed, I put in a challenge on the stand-side touchline in front of the Hearts dug-out and as the free kick was being taken by them I could hear their coach, Walter Borthwick, giving me dog's abuse and reminding me that I was 'nothing but a cripple'. I was so caught up in the game, not to mention surprised, that I just carried on playing and didn't return the compliment.

The game was fairly uneventful and finished 0–0, but as we headed down the tunnel all hell broke loose. Alex MacDonald, who was Hearts boss at the time, remarked to Mo Johnston, who wasn't long at Ibrox after his shock summer signing, 'You shouldn't even be at this club', or words to that effect. Never one for thinking first, wee Mo swung a punch and it was seconds out. Things were already out of hand when I spotted Borthwick coming towards me. I remembered his comments, but decided that it wasn't worth the hassle getting involved (honest!). The next thing, he had made a dive towards Souness, who was on the other side of a police barrier at the tunnel. I grabbed a hold of him, pushed him away and he connected with a kick to the leg, fortunately not doing any lasting damage. I then connected with a retaliatory volley between the legs which dropped him in a heap. Our kitman, Jimmy Bell, helped break things up and even though there were a few coppers around they simply split it up and ordered us to our separate dressing-rooms. It had all happened within a few seconds and there were still players coming up the tunnel so it was probably difficult for them to identify the culprits.

Graeme Souness, who was banned to the stand at this time and couldn't get through the police barriers, either to stop it or help us out, said: 'Right, I want everyone who was involved in that to put their hands up.' Mo, myself, Ian Ferguson and Jimmy all stuck our mitts in the air, expecting a rollicking over discipline and such like. Instead, the Gaffer came round and shook all our hands. 'Well done, lads, that was brilliant,' he said. 'That's what I want at this club, everyone sticking together and fighting each other's battles.'

Chapter Eight

The Famous Five

My long-awaited Old Firm début came in August 1988 and what a start it was. The Ibrox scoreboard, at the end of that near-perfect 90 minutes, read – RANGERS 5 CELTIC 1, as we handed out a real thrashing to our oldest rivals. Every Rangers fan who has ever kicked a ball dreams as a kid of playing in what is *the* derby match and famous round the world. But to play in your first and finish with a scoreline like that is beyond words.

Graeme Souness that day gave a team talk which I had never heard anything like before or since. When he first arrived at Ibrox, he tried to play down the importance of these fixtures, saying that it was just two points, like any other match. But I think he quickly discovered that he was wrong. Victories against your oldest rivals can make or break your season and they mean everything to the punters.

The religious, historical and cultural differences between the two communities in Nothern Ireland and in the West of Scotland, where there are strong Irish connections, are well documented. And even though the barrier between the two sides is one that some people would prefer wasn't there, it exists, and on no occasion is this more evident than at an Old Firm match.

The banning of alcohol from Scottish matches, after the pitched battle of the 1980 Scottish Cup final between the two clubs, has certainly meant there isn't the same level of drink-fuelled antagonism on the terracings or in the stands. But for some fans it's still a hate-filled 90 minutes and I don't think that will ever change. Nor will the involvement, willingly or otherwise, of the two clubs.

Before that historic match Souness pointed out to us just why we have a portrait of the Queen hanging in the the dressing-room, why our fans fly the Union Jack and the traditions of the club and why Celtic fans fly tricolours and sing IRA songs. Now, he was wasting his breath with the Scots lads like myself, Ally and Fergie who were well aware of that, but by the time he had finished putting over various points and explained all this in the context of what a victory would mean to our fans, even the English players like Ray Wilkins went down the tunnel with steam coming out of their ears. I'd never seen him and Gary Stevens so pumped up for a match.

It all seemed to be going wrong for a brief moment when Frank McAvennie opened the scoring, until we equalised and from then on it was one-way traffic. Ally McCoist scored two, with Ray Wilkins, Kevin Drinkell and – who else? – Mark Walters notching the others.

You always enjoy Old Firm matches if you've won, but normally after the match, because it's just so hectic and demanding for the full 90 minutes. This was unique because we were 5–1 up with plenty of time left on the clock and we had a chance to savour every moment. It's one of my happiest memories.

At that point Souness brought himself on and started to knock the ball about. It was entertaining stuff, but it really took the pressure off Celtic – there were definitely a few more goals left in us and our fans could see that. It was a great chance for us to wipe out Celtic's 7–1 victory in the Old Firm League Cup final of 1957, which would have really made the punters happy, but it was still the biggest winning margin in over 20 years. Celtic had totally gone by then and their players were just desperate to get off the park as quickly as possible.

Unlike some Old Firm games, when you get a fair amount of banter or backchat between the opposing players on the field, depending on how the match is going, there was nothing to say. In the 1989 Cup final when we blew the Treble and Celtic took a bit of revenge for the 5–1 gubbing, I can always remember late in the game, when we were out of it, Peter Grant knocking the ball past me and having a chuckle as he did so. There wasn't much I could say at the time but I like to think we've had the last laugh for the past six seasons and it certainly wasn't as a result of anything we'd done during the 5–1 match – it's never been my style to rub it in where fellow professionals are concerned. You just get on with it. You know they're having a hard enough time, although perhaps we should sometimes make more capital out of our victories, the way Celtic do when they get a result against us.

After the match we were back out on the pitch doing a warm-down and still on a huge high. There was all sort of rubbish swirling round the stadium and Ray, who had shown such skill, class and timing to score the goal of the match, with an incredible volley, managed to get a bin bag caught round his ankles and crashed to the track in a heap, flat on his face, to general hysterics from the lads.

Anyway it was a great Old Firm Ibrox début and I'm pleased to say that since then I've been on more than my fair share of winning sides against Celtic and enjoyed every second.

The same season we made it back-to-back victories at Ibrox when we gubbed them 4–1. We could hardly believe it when, after going behind to an early goal again, this time from Chris Morris, we went on to run up another score like that. We were all hoping we could make it five again, or maybe go one better, but we were absolutely delighted with the final result, especially Terry Butcher, Mark Walters, who scored two including one from the penalty spot, and Ian Ferguson, who got on the scoresheet that day.

You're always more hyped up for those games than normal and on one occasion at Parkhead the Doc had me breathing in and out of a paper bag to try and calm me down. I felt daft and the rest of the lads were killing themselves, but it worked and I managed to save some energy for the match.

In time you realise that you have to be up for it without exhausting yourself. You learn to relax a bit more, not think about it too much and then get yourself tuned in about an hour before kick-off. If you're from Glasgow or the West of Scotland and your family are at the game, getting a decent result is even more important as you know the type of stick they'll have to take when they get to work on a Monday if you don't.

Another Old Firm high came in the 1992 Ne'erday match at Parkhead. I came off the bench just before Mark Hateley put us ahead from the penalty spot after Coisty had been brought down. And on a gloomy and wet afternoon, with the light fading, the brightest thing in the stadium was my grin after grabbing goal number three. I picked up the ball just over the halfway line and pushed even further forward. I think the Celtic players were expecting a wide pass, but instead I cut outside and let loose with a 20-yard shot which came off the inside of the post on its way past Gordon Marshall. I made a dash for the Rangers end and jumped the advertising boards before wheeling round and back on to the pitch, deciding a booking for leaving the field without the referee's permission might not be the ideal way to finish my celebrations.

Another New Year's Day which the team and the punters won't forget in a hurry came more recently, in January 1994, when we found ourselves three up after half an hour. It looked as though another hammering was on the cards, but in the end we had to settle for 4–2 as Celtic pulled back a late goal to give the scoreline a bit of respectability. Alexei Mikhailitchenko got two, Mark Hateley, who had a good record against Celtic, hit another and Oleg Kuznetsov blasted in a superb volley. Another reason that game sticks out in my mind was the mini-pitch invasion after we'd scored our third. I always turn to see our fans' reaction when we score rather than the players' celebrations, and the place was bouncing. But my happy reverie was disturbed when out of the corner of my eye I spotted a Celtic fan on the trackside vault off a stretcher which was taking him to the medical room and run towards our keeper Ally Maxwell. Because of the noise and the fact that we were so far ahead, Maxie wasn't paying too much attention to what was happening and it was only when he saw the look on my face as I sprinted towards them both that he turned round and clocked the guy and we both grappled him to the ground, gently of course, before the police carted him off.

It's something I've never had to deal with before, although in England, pitch invasions are a fairly regular occurrence at some grounds, but I'll tell you, I'd rather have the St Andrew's Ambulance first aiders treat me any day if that's the sort of recovery you can make, from lying flat out on a stretcher to being able to beat Linford Christie in a 100-metre sprint.

There have been plenty of other Old Firm League matches where I've ended up on the winning side, but although they're great to win, you get another three chances to make up for a defeat during the course of a season. Cup ties become even more crucial and there's no prizes for guessing that the Scottish Cup semi-final in March 1992 is top of the list of successes.

We had lost ten days previously to Celtic with Charlie Nicholas and Gerry Creaney bagging the goals in their 2–0 Ibrox victory. Judging by some of the reports in the press afterwards you would have thought they had won the League. They were obviously on a high after that and a few comments from Tony Mowbray, among others, in a couple of articles really got our backs up. It was bad enough losing to them, but when they started making all sorts of predictions for the Cup clash, it fired us up even more.

Normally there's a longer gap between the Old Firm League matches, but with the Cup-tie just over a week away, we were delighted to get a second bite so soon. Remember, we had lost to Celtic in the Scottish Cup quarter-final the previous season and our record in the competition was pretty poor over the years, so although it's hard to believe with all the success we've had since, we were probably the underdogs at Hampden. But we all sensed that we would beat them. It didn't matter how or under what circumstances, we just had a feeling in the camp that we could pull this one off, recognising it as a great opportunity to get our own back.

It was also the first time Walter had been in charge for the Cup campaign. Graeme always took the attitude that the trophy was there for you, but lucky teams could win it and the best team in the country was always the one which won the League. Walter put more emphasis on doing well in the competition, although he saw the League as the major prize too.

We went into the game with our confidence high, but six minutes into the match it looked as if things were going horribly wrong. Celtic winger Joe Miller, a former team-mate of David Robertson's at Aberdeen, had given Robbo a bit of a tough time in the previous game and in the run-up to the next clash Robbo took a lot of stick from the lads and Archie kidding him on about how he could come out of wee Joe's pocket now and 'Aye, you and Joe Miller must be the best of buddies'. As it happened he and Joe were quite friendly during their Pittodrie days, but you could see him reacting to this and gradually getting more wound up and probably thinking, 'We'll see how long he lasts this time.'

About six minutes was the answer. From the first whistle Robbo was desperate to get a hit on Joe and while fans were still taking their seats, he was on his way back up the tunnel. Maybe it was our own fault, we shouldn't have wound him up as much, but suddenly we had to re-jig the defence and our backs were to the wall – with 84 minutes left to play.

The Celtic fans, of course, were delighted, anticipating an easy victory, but fortunately it didn't turn out that way. I went to left back and Nigel Spackman moved into centre-half with Coisty up front on his own and Ian Durrant playing off him. And from there we played some great football in atrocious conditions. It was absolutely pouring down and my dad and brother, who were sitting in the front row of the stand, got absolutely soaked to the skin along with thousands of others.

A lot of fans got flu that night, but I don't think they minded after Coisty grabbed a great opportunist goal. Stuart McCall supplied a defence-splitting pass and Ally finished really well into the right-hand corner of Pat Bonnar's net. From then on it was a real battle. Celtic hit the woodwork a couple of times and we were really under pressure, but there were ten very happy guys when the final whistle went.

To win the game after playing so long with ten men in those conditions was a great achievement. But in wider terms it was even more important. It gave us the chance to overcome our Cup jinx and win the trophy for the first time in 11 years, to clinch the

Double and set us up to win all three trophies the following season, followed by another two trophies in the season after that.

We still had it all to do against Airdrie in May, but that night we felt as if we had won the Cup. And there was no one happier than Robbo. He was sitting in the dressing-room when he heard the roar go up and assumed Celtic had scored. So he was greatly relieved not to have cost us the tie, especially with our previously poor record in the Cup. A lot of people had written us off, but the boys were made of sterner stuff and reacted well to some derogatory remarks. Everyone stood up and was counted – they had to be. It's the manager's job to motivate players, but when the opposition do it for him through the press, it makes his life easier.

Of course it wasn't the last time we were to beat the Celts with ten men. Although most of our successes in my time with the club have come at Parkhead, with guys like Nigel Spackman and Terry Hurlock both making scoring Old Firm débuts there, Ibrox has been a relatively happy hunting ground for Celtic. So when we were drawn against them in the League Cup semi-final two seasons ago their confidence was fairly high, especially as, for the first time, their fans had the whole of the Govan stand as well as the Broomloan. And they were delighed when we found ourselves down to ten men early in the match after Pieter Huistra clashed with Tom Boyd and was red-carded. But once again, we proved equal to the challenge.

I was sorry to hear about Parkhead defender Mike Galloway's terrible car crash recently and I was gutted for him and his family. But that night he was the scapegoat for their defeat. He had a tendency to overdo things at the back sometimes instead of clearing his lines. Ian Durrant, who was buzzing that night, must have read the script because he was on hand to rob Mike of the ball and deliver a perfect cross for Mark Hateley to fire home from close range and dump them out of the Cup.

Like Davie Robertson before him, Pieter was a relieved man that his rash behaviour wasn't as costly as it could have been. The circumstances don't matter. It was definitely a bit stupid of him to swing at Boyd.

Another Ibrox moment to savour was in November 1989 when Mo Johnston scored his first Old Firm goal. He had played against Celtic at Parkhead beforehand and took stick from both sets of fans for not scoring and missing a few chances. In those scarf-burning and season ticket returning days there were still Rangers fans who believed that Mo couldn't or wouldn't be able to score a goal against his old club. With the light fading – there were just two minutes left on the clock that dull afternoon – he proved that he could and would. A great first touch set up a shooting chance and he placed the low shot out of the keeper's reach in the bottom corner and was then booked for celebrating in front of the Copland Road stand.

The wee man was desperate to score for us and, having won over some fans with a valuable goal against Aberdeen a few weeks before, he gained the respect of many more with that strike. Even if you ask him now, I think he'll still tell you that that goal meant a lot to him and he would rate it as one of his most important strikes. You could understand his joy after all the hassle and problems his arrival at Ibrox brought. In the first few months after he signed all the cars at Ibrox were regularly checked for bombs and for the first time ever they were locked inside the stadium on the track instead of on Edmiston Drive. And when we arrived back from Italy days after his arrival we had to leave Glasgow airport by a side entrance after a bus had collected us on the tarmac straight off the plane because of the threats against Mo and the club. There were still those who didn't take to him, but there's no doubt he gave 100 per cent in every game he played for Rangers.

Playing for either half of the Old Firm is a rewarding exper- ience in financial and footballing terms, but it also brings its own particular pressures too, as were highlighted by Mo's controversial signing. Off and on the park every move made by players is scrutinised by fans and press and the stories tend to grow arms and legs by the time they've done the rounds of every pub in the city. Rivalry between the two sets of fans can also cause problems. Players in Dundee or Edinburgh are in a similar situation, but what sets Glasgow apart is the sectarian divide which is as wide as ever.

One incident which sums up the inbred attitudes that still prevail happened to me in the city centre one evening. After a night out with the boys, I was heading home, so I jumped into the first taxi I saw and asked the driver to take me to Newton Mearns on the south side of the city. A couple of minutes later, it became obvious I was being taken for a ride and I asked the guy which route he was taking.

'You're in my car, you'll go where I take you,' was the helpful response.

'Stop the car.'

No reply, until finally we screech to a halt and Glasgow's happiest taxi driver demands 75p, before finally unlocking the doors when it's clear he's got no chance.

Less than amused, I clock the rosary beads hanging from the rear view mirror and realise why the guy has just called me a 'Dirty, Orange B------'.

A friendly kick at his door doesn't help the situation, but he roars away and I head off down Renfield Street. A minute later there's a diesel engine getting pretty close and I turn to find the taxi from hell is on the pavement behind me and not likely to stop. Fortunately, I managed to duck into a shop doorway as the hackney flashed by.

Maybe the guy just wanted to scare me, but on the other hand he would probably have been on free drinks all night in his local if he had run me down. It's crazy, but that's the way it is. The only thing which set me apart from the guy's other passengers was the fact that I played for Rangers, and that was enough for him to try and rob me blind, then pick a fight and try and run me over! And it's not just Celtic fans either. Your own supporters can be just as bad, if not worse, because you see more of them as you don't tend to be in opposition territory too often. Sometimes you go to supporters functions and you'll have fans who can't handle their drink criticising your team-mates. Fair enough, you play for a big club and to a certain extent you're public property. But I can't handle too much of that. At first you can politely disagree, but if it starts to get nasty you have to walk away. You can bet if you started telling them what you thought of some of their pals they would be the first to get upset.

Don't get me wrong, with 99 per cent of the supporters at functions it's a pleasure to talk to them and the crack can be brilliant. But it's the minority who let the others down. If you play for the Old Firm it's part of your job to be able to handle off-the-field pressure like that and I have to be honest and say that playing for a reasonably successful side means you rarely get problems. But things got a bit out of hand during the disastrous spell in 1991, just before Graeme Souness left for Liverpool, when we had three players sent off as we crashed two weeks on the trot at Parkhead.

I was still carrying an Achilles injury and resting up for that final do-or-die match with Aberdeen, and Ian Durrant was also still on the way back. For the first game we both headed for Blantyre, met up with my mate Big Stan, Willie Black and few of the other lads, had a few beers and then squeezed on to a slightly over-booked minibus that looked like some of these trains you see in India with bodies hanging off the sides and on the roof.

On the terracing at the Rangers end we had already been asked for tickets for the second match before, at five minutes to three, a guy tapped us on the shoulder and says, 'Aren't you playing today?' Good guess, pal. Hang on till we jump the barrier and rip off these denim warm-up suits.

Pretty soon it was your worst nightmare. We're down to nine men and Celtic are three up. We were both gutted, but did the decent thing and went back to Blantyre for a sing-song.

The following week, like everyone else, we assumed things could only get better. Wrong again. We were in a well-known pub in Bridgeton, which it's safe to say is a fairly secure place to be with a Rangers scarf on. Coisty was back after his fall-out with Souness over a trip to the Cheltenham Gold Cup (he should have played in the first match, too, in my opinion) and John Spencer was also playing. We really should have got something out of that game, but pretty soon it was Nightmare On Janefield Street II.

The fans were sick, which I could understand, but you have to take the rough with the smooth. If they had suffered the way Celtic fans had as they went through a barren spell, then they might have had an excuse for branding everyone from the chairman down 'a disgrace'. But it just shows you how important these two games were to the fans.

Back in the pub afterwards the fans were really good and tried to lift me and themselves saying, 'Come on, Bomber, cheer up, give us a song.' We were drowning our sorrows when a guy came over selling space on one of these football sweep cards. I asked how many he had left and on finding out it was only half a dozen said, 'I'll take the rest then', thinking I was doing the guy a favour. Unfortunately I hadn't read the card. 'Oh, you're taking that Celtic mob then,' he snarled and started swearing his head off at me. Finally, I'd had enough. I ripped his card up and told him I couldn't believe what he was coming away with.

It calmed down until we were leaving and the same guy and his wife started in on me again. One of my mates pulled me outside and not a moment too soon. As soon as the doors shut there was sound like a milk float crashing as bottles and glasses started to fly. The rest of the clientele were showing their disapproval of this lunatic's idea of hospitality.

It's a funny game all right, but sometimes it's no laughing matter.

Despite the tensions that surround the two clubs, the Old Firm players in general tend to get on well off the field, without actually making a point of socialising together. There have been a couple who wouldn't be your ideal choice of companion for a night out, but then again their own team-mates probably feel the same way and it's got nothing to do with the colour of strip they wear. But if we bump into each other at functions then we'll have a drink and a chat together.

Pat Bonnar and I made an appearance for charity a few years back and spent a pleasant enough couple of hours. Not long afterwards we were playing against each other and it was total hatred from the first whistle to the last. You just want to do each other, simple as that. That's your job and it's not like playing for any other team. It's Rangers v Celtic, it's deadly serious and you're not going to take second best. The two of us were calling each other for everything and got booked for our trouble, but the next time we met it was first names again instead of unrepeatable ones and it was all forgotten.

It's good that you've got guys who can accept that it's just the match and who calm down after it although usually there's a cooling-off period. Unlike any other fixture there isn't usually the chance for a post-match beer in the players' lounge. If you've lost the last thing you want to see is a lot of grinning faces and vice versa. So we're not exactly best of buddies, but there is a respect there. You know that you're both playing for the two biggest and most high-profile clubs in Scotland and you've a lot in common in terms of being under the spotlight in this city most of the time.

An incident I'm constantly reminded of was the match when I congratulated a Tommy Coyne goal a bit over-zealously and tried to make sure he stayed in the goalmouth for longer than required. I had missed the ball in the middle of the park, Celtic broke, fired it wide and Tommy was on the end of it to finish from close range. As he ran behind the goal line and into the net I caught up with him and connected with my knee. A second later I was wishing I had connected a bit harder because he didn't stay down for long and was up and and away a second later. My old mate Gerry McNee didn't approve of this challenge either and reckoned I should have been sent off. Cheers, Gerry, nice to get a neutral opinion. Though to be fair it was probably worth a booking, though no serious damage was done.

Tommy is, of course, an old team-mate from my Dens days, and it wasn't really fair on him, but I was raging about the goal. The red mist had descended and, to be honest, I couldn't even have told you which Celtic player was in our net. All I saw was red . . . then green and white.

Chapter Nine

Bombed Out

After my initial success with Rangers, the lowest point of my Ibrox career came on 12 October 1990 when Graeme Souness dropped me from the side for the first time – to make way for the former Dynamo Kiev star Oleg Kuznetsov. I'd missed a few games in the past, through injuries, or sat out a few on the bench because of tactical switches on the manager's part. But now I had to cope with being replaced while I was fully fit and on form and I have to admit now that I thought my days were numbered.

Oleg had starred against us in a pre-season friendly and arrived nearly three months later for his much-heralded début against St Mirren at Ibrox.

I wasn't upset when the club signed him, but I was gutted that Friday afternoon when Souness called me into his office and broke the bad news. I had been playing really well, having taken over the number six shirt vacated by Terry Butcher who had played his last game for the club nearly a month beforehand. I could understand a big signing like Oleg having to play in his chosen position, which was in central defence, but I had hoped, in fact probably expected, that he would then tell me I was playing elsewhere in the back four or in a midfield role as I had done in the past.

Instead, he declared that the next day I would be off to Love Street with the reserves. I left his office and headed back down the marble staircase absolutely gutted. When you're not fit or you're not playing well, you have to accept that someone else is likely to take your place, but not when you are raring to go at the start of the season with the League campaign only just begun, and the League Cup and Europe looming large.

I don't think I did too good a job of disguising my disappointment and when I passed the Gaffer later in the day he told me: 'There's still a place here for you.' He was obviously trying to lift my spirits a bit, but in the back of my mind I already knew that a big-money signing like Oleg, who was also our first Russian player, was obviously likely to hold down that defensive position for years to come and my own future might not be looking too rosy, despite Souness's words. At Paisley the next day, John McGregor, the reserve coach, asked me if I wanted to be skipper and for the first time in my entire career I said no and told him to give it to someone else, one of the younger players. John probably thought, and rightly so, that it was a bad attitude and example for a senior player to set, but being honest, I couldn't have cared less. Now I'm involved in the coaching side myself I realise how difficult it must have been for John on occasions, not only having to motivate his youngsters, but also gee up older players who have either been dropped or are on their way back from injury.

But after a nightmare 90 minutes, John did managed to put a smile on my face for the first time in two days. The dressing-room at Love Street was roasting hot and with the help of a couple of other lads I had managed to prop open the windows with a wooden wedge and let some air in. Now, we had just lost a goal in the last minute to draw 2–2 with the Saints when John came in with the steam coming out of his ears. He was looking for something to take his frustrations out on and unfortunately, on his way past, he punched the piece of wood out of the way and got ready to tell the lads exactly what he thought. When it came down and slammed on his thumb the most comical thing was the expressions on the team's faces, including guys like John Spencer and Gary McSwegan, as they tried not to laugh. The place would have collapsed otherwise, but the boys knew better than to upset John, who's not known as Mad Dog McGregor, for nothing. It was a little bit of light relief for me after my recent mood.

I was still more or less convinced that my time at Ibrox was over. Bigger stars had come and gone through the front door at Ibrox and Souness was always on the lookout to try and strengthen the squad by a bit of wheeling and dealing in the transfer market, so there was no reason I should have regarded myself as any different in that respect. But although I was prepared to consider the doomsday scenario, I was also ready to knuckle down, do my best in the reserves, if that was what I had to do, and wait for another chance.

Fortunately for me, and very unfortunately for Oleg, I didn't have long to wait. After a terrific debut against St Mirren, his season was over almost as soon as it had begun at McDiarmid Park the following week. He fell awkwardly after a challenge from a St Johnstone player, was carried off and knee ligament damage was confirmed the next day. You never like to see any player injured, even if it benefits you, and I was sorry for the big man, particularly as I had had similar bad luck myself over the years.

Although I had been upset at my own situation and place within the side, from the team's point of view I was *glad* Kuznetsov had signed. Although I wasn't involved in Rangers' European clash with Dynamo Kiev a few years before, Coisty had told me that the big man had proved to a real hard case with plenty of aggression and skill to match. You could see even in the pre-season friendly when Oleg ran the length of the park and scored at the Copland Road end that he was a very good, strong player. He was a real class act with Kiev and also starred in Russia's European Championship-winning side.

His injury and the long-term rehabilitation it required meant that I was given the chance I had wanted and the only snag after that was the Achilles injury which grew gradually worse throughout the season and forced me to miss the run-in to the title decider with the Dons. I was back in for our clash with Red Star in Belgrade and, looking back, my return virtually ended Oleg's Ibrox career.

Oleg spent a lot of time working with physiotherapist Bill Collins, who was eventually to join Rangers, at Bangour Hospital in West Lothian and gradually made his comeback in September 1991 against Dundee United, playing with his former team-mate Alexei Mikhailitchenko, who had signed from Sampdoria, for the first time since their Kiev days. At the start of that 1991/92 season, Scott Nisbet claimed a place in the centre of defence beside Richard Gough and was our best player for a long period. After my Achilles tendon had blown up I was out for a lengthy period. My comeback took place in the Skol Cup semi-final against Hibs on 25 September with Oleg and Alexei missing through international commitments. I then made a few sporadic appearances and spent some time on the bench. After Nissy injured himself, Oleg and Goughie paired up until the Ukrainian was sent off against Airdrie at Broomfield in January. Then I was finally back at full fitness and once again grabbed the chance to stake my claim in what was to prove to be our first Double-winning side in years. I was playing in midfield that day before returning to defensive duties from then on. I was also back in the starting line-up after a lot of substitute appearances, including one against Celtic a few days before when I had scored our third, and my first, Old Firm goal.

Although Oleg had regained his fitness and played well in several matches around that time, he was never really the same player afterwards and didn't play as much of a part in first team duties as would have been expected.

After a few seasons in the wilderness, he eventually moved to Israel before returning to Kiev shortly afterwards, though not before scoring a superb volley in a 4–2 Ne'erday victory over Celtic which is certainly something he'll be remembered for. His departure was a real shame as he was a fine player, and his signing was a bold move on Souness's part. It was just a pity we didn't get to see the best of him.

As I've said, my return to action was instantly forgettable as Keith Wright scored the only goal of the game to send the Hibees into the Skol Cup final and end our near-domination of the tournament. Apart from the 1989 extra-time defeat in the final against the Dons, it was our first defeat in the competion in six years, and it wasn't an ideal return from my own point of view.

Three in a row . . . the side which snatched the title on the last day of the season at Ibrox in 1991. (*Mike Schofield/Rangers News*)

Glory day . . . celebrating my unforgettable goal in the 1992 Ne'erday victory over Celtic. (*Daily Record*)

10 out of 10 . . . myself, Andy and Big Slim were the only three who played in all our European matches in 1992/93. (*Daily Record*)

Champions again . . . lap of honour at Broomfield in May 1993.

Teddy bears' picnic . . . McCoist, Brown and Gough at another Ibrox title-winning party in 1993. (*Daily Record*)

Treble yell . . . it's party time at Parkhead as we clinch the Scottish Cup with a victory over Aberdeen in May 1993. (*Daily Record*)

Air we go . . . rising to the challenge against Leeds United's Eric Cantona and Lee Chapman at Elland Road. (*Rangers News*)

Heart-breaker . . . the goal which knocked the Jam Tarts out of the Cup in March 1994. (*Daily Record*)

Ya beauty . . . the expression on my face tells you we've scored.
(*Rangers News*)

Warming up . . . and keeping out the cold at an Ibrox training session.

Daddy's girls . . . Lauren (left) and Megan.

On the mend . . . with Lauren after her op. (*Daily Record*)

We also lost out in Europe. I sat on the bench for our first leg tie against Sparta Prague and returned for the home leg which saw Nissy and Andy Goram singled out for criticism after a comedy of errors which helped Sparta go through on the away goals rule after a 2–2 draw on aggregate. It was hardly an auspicious start to Walter's first Euro campaign but, fortunately, things were going well in the League and in the Scottish Cup we were to make an impact for the first time.

Having grabbed my place back in January, I was in the line-up when we set off on the road to Hampden with a 1–0 victory over Aberdeen. Ally McCoist grabbed the all-important goal, but the hero that night was Andy Goram who had a superb last-gasp save from Brian Irvine which put us through to the next round.

It looked as if the old Cup jinx was back in the next round when we went a goal down to Motherwell at Ibrox, but Alexei Mikhailitchenko hit back with two great goals to put us into the quarter-finals against St Johnstone. Here, McCoist, Gough and Hateley bagged the goals to set up the unforgettable semi-final at Hampden against Celtic. Despite being down to ten men we held on for a famous win, again thanks to Super Ally.

In the League we more or less wrapped it up at Tannadice. Miko grabbed our first goal and I blasted in number two in the 68th minute. Such was the rivalry between Dundee and Dundee United, I always loved getting one over them and Jim McLean and you can see just how much I enjoyed that strike by the picture on the front cover of this book. Miko's earlier goal in that match also marked our 100th in the League that season. It was the first time since the Premier Division was set up that any team reached such a milestone and it also made us the Division's all-time highest scoring side.

The following week a 4–0 win over St Mirren at home completed the formalities. The title was ours again. I was to miss out on victories over Motherwell and Aberdeen, but I was there for a 1–1 draw with Hearts in a live TV match when we picked up the League Championship trophy.

It was great to have another title-winning party, but even better was that final game at Pittodrie where we finished with a bit of style and two goals from Coisty which looked great from my seat in the stand. Unfortunately, we weren't able to see an action replay of them as the only cameras there were for Aberdeen's own purposes.

Before that game I travelled with the squad to our usual base at the Holiday Inn at Dyce, which was normally quiet and ideal for preparation for what was always a big game at Pittodrie. But to the management's horror there was a graduation ball, or some other big do, on at the hotel that Friday night and the place was pandemonium. I was allowed to enjoy the party atmosphere because I wasn't playing, but I wasn't alone and some of my team-mates, who'll remain nameless, also joined in and had a few beers, even though Archie was enforcing his own personal prohibition act and guarding all the corridors and checking rooms for any sign of illicit booze. It may sound a bit unprofessional, but we had worked really hard to win the title and the pressure was off, so we were determined to enjoy that last League experience.

Ironically, the only player who was named in the next day's investigation was Sandy Roberston, who was one of the few innocent parties. He had been shopped to Archie. After the manager had given his team talk and left the dressing-room, Archie rounded on the team and said, 'Right, every one of you, I know what you were up to last night. And you, Robertson, what were you thinking of ordering chicken wings and a pint of lager at midnight last night?'

'It wasn't, it was only a blackcurrant and lemonade,' Sandy protested weakly.

'It disnae matter, you shouldn't have been eating at that time of night either,' screamed Archie. 'And I'll warn you now, I know you were all drinking last night and you had better put on a good show today – or else,' he added ominously.

Of course we won 2–0. Coisty scored two wonder goals and had the last word as usual. After finding the net with a 25-yard volley which followed a magnificent chip from the edge of the box, he sprinted across to the dugout where myself and the coaching staff and subs were and, wearing a huge grin, shouted, 'Those pints last night seem to have done the trick.' We were all in stitches and even Archie was seen to have a quiet smirk to himself.

Aberdeen trips over the years have provided a few more laughs. Not long after Terry Hurlock signed for us he was rooming with me the night before the game and as he relaxed with a bit of late-night telly he shouted, 'Bomber, c'mere! What this bleedin' nonsense on the telly?' He was watching some Gaelic programme and was wondering if everyone in Aberdeen spoke like that.

'Don't worry,' I told him. 'We don't understand a word of it either.'

On another occasion, Paul Rideout, who went on to score Everton's winning FA Cup final goal last season, was rooming with me at the same hotel. He wasn't playing and ended up having a late night in the bar with Mark Hateley, who was also out. Big Mark had seen him off in the drinking stakes and Paul finally got me out of my kip in the early hours. In between him apologising to me and the curtains for waking us up, I finally got the light out again and spent five minutes, being more accustomed to the dark than he was, watching him grope his way round the room for the toilet.

Finally I had to show him the way. Then I switched the light off and got my head down again. The only problem was I hadn't switched the light on in the bathroom. Ten minutes passed before I heard, 'Help. Help. Bomber, I'm locked in, help me!' I had to bite my pillow to cover my laughter before finally rescuing him from a bathroom that had never been locked anyway.

I didn't find it nearly as funny in that Double-winning season when I feared I might miss out on the Scottish Cup final. I had aggravated a calf injury in the final home game and it looked for a while as if I might miss the Cup final. But the two-week gap between the last League fixture and the final which was introduced for the first time by the SFA allowed me to scrape through.

At the time, Ian Ferguson was the only guy in the dressing-room with a winner's badge and after the disappointment of losing out in 1989, there was no way I wanted to miss this one. Bill Collins, our physio at the time, worked me really hard down at

Turnberry and the day before the game I threw myself into a training game at Ibrox, diving all over the place. I was so relieved to get through it and pass that fitness test.

The manager had said not to worry, he would look after me if I missed out, but I wanted to be there and win a medal through my own efforts. And getting our hands on that particular piece of silver, 11 years after the Gers had last won it, meant a lot to all concerned.

That summer I went to South Africa, where I had a great time at Sun City at my mate Jackie Potter's place, and in Johannesburg, where I met loads of exiled supporters.

Shortly afterward, Di and I were on holiday in Florida where I met Andy Smith who had scored Airdrie's goal in the Cup final and was out there to get married. I don't think Airdrie really had high expectations of winning, but he was just delighted to have made it that far and to have scored a goal in the final.

But after my fitness battles and the ongoing fight to keep my place and deny guys like Oleg, and other younger stars, the chance to put me back on the bench, the smell of success was even sweeter.

Chapter Ten

Durranty

One of the most harrowing afternoons I've ever had on a football pitch came on 8 October 1988 at Pittodrie. Neale Cooper, Graham Souness's latest capture, scored on his début, which normally would have been worth a headline or two, especially as he was back on familiar territory having starred with Aberdeen's all-conquering side of the early Eighties. But instead, it was his namesake and former team-mate, Neil Simpson, who found himself on all the back pages as one horrifying moment changed two players' careers forever.

We lost the match, with Charlie Nicholas scoring the Dons' winner, but for once we didn't care about the result after the infamous incident which nearly ended Ian Durrant's career with shattered knee ligaments. Quite simply, the tackle inflicted on Ian that day by the Aberdeen midfielder had horrendous repercussions.

I was just feet away from the incident when it happened and saw it as though it were in slow motion. To see the wee man's knee buckle sideways as the tackle came in sent a shiver right through me. I was shocked and as Ian collapsed I went up to Simpson and grabbed a hold of him, but I was so stunned I didn't know what to say. I just stared at him and I don't think he could comprehend the damage he'd done either.

Just before, he'd taken a knock which had obviously fired him up for the next tackle. But ironically, two seconds before they clashed, the ref blew for a free-kick to us – just too late, as Simpson had already steamed in.

If Ian had had his foot off the deck he might have picked up a sore knock, but not anywhere near as bad as the eventual damage caused by having his full weight on the knee as the tackle came right through him. There wasn't even a stretcher at Pittodrie, so he had to be lifted off in great pain.

Having had plenty of ops and injuries myself, I knew how much worry and frustration could be involved, though never to that extent. But for a youngster in his early twenties to end up living a three-year nightmare just at the moment when he was producing some of his best-ever form was nothing short of tragic.

After the initial pain there were so many doubts, even among the medical people at Ibrox, over whether he would ever play again, never mind come back to his best, it was such a bad injury. One of the docs reckoned the injury was more like what you would expect after a road accident rather than a football injury.

To this day, Aberdeen fans still boo Durranty as though he's done something wrong and was in any way responsible for the decline in Neil Simpson's career after that incident. I can't understand that attitude at all. The hatred spouted by those morons is a total disgrace. Whether or not Simpson was affected by it is a different issue. He's the one who cost Ian so many vital years of his career . . . medals, Scotland caps, goals and glory. I have to admit that even now I couldn't sit down and chat to Neil Simpson. That may sound bitter, but I can't forget what happened that day and even if one of my own team-mates did something similar I would lose a lot of respect for them. You could see in the TV pictures and photographs of his tackle there was hate in his eyes that day. I know football is a physical game and it's inevitable that people are going to get hurt on occasions, but that was quite literally over the top.

Aberdeen have been our main rivals in recent seasons and at that time we were winning championships again and they were desperate to snatch something from us, so you're always going to get that bit of needle which happens at all levels in football. There was more of a physical side to those matches around that time than there was in the Old Firm games which had a bit of football in them.

If there's a physical battle you want to win it and boys like Neil Simpson had that quality, which you could also see in Neale Cooper when he joined us. They were brought up with that during the Dons' Eighties revival under Alex Ferguson. But until that moment I wouldn't have described him as a dirty player.

As soon as we came off the pitch, to a man we walked into the dressing-room and asked how Durranty was. Then he had to endure the three-hour coach journey from Aberdeen to Glasgow on the back seat. It must have been torture for him. You could see just how serious it was by the faces of the management and Doc Cruickshank. But when we heard the full extent of the damage we couldn't believe it. We played Aberdeen again two weeks after that in the League Cup final and we were glad to win the game, thanks to a late goal from Ally, after Davie Dodds scored two for the Dons, but there was a hollow feeling to it.

The memory of that incident will always stay with me. I don't know any other players, apart from Ally, who could put up with an injury like that. Ian would come into Ibrox full of smiles as usual during his rehabilitation period. You would have a knock which might keep you out for a couple of weeks, but if you even thought about moaning about it you only had to look at him with a calliper on his knee and massive op scars and you realised how insignificant your own troubles were. 'What are you worried about?' he'd say. 'You'll be back in a couple of weeks . . . I'll be back in a couple of years.' Things like that really stopped you feeling sorry for yourself.

Of course the road back to full fitness was never a smooth one. We all had a real scare one day when, after a first operation, Durranty just seemed to buckle on the Albion training pitch and did some more damage to his knee. It was then that they decided he should go to America for more treatment, a revolutionary transplant operation to strengthen the knee. At that time people, as they had throughout, were saying, 'This is his last chance. He'll never be back', and so on. The rumour factory, which is always on overtime where Old Firm players are concerned, was convinced that this time it was all over.

One day we were soaking in the the big communal bath at Ibrox after training and Phil Boersma, the physio/trainer at the time, declared, 'We reckon Durranty's finished, he'll never kick a ball again.' Coisty, who loves the wee man, was in tears, and I wasn't far behind. I had a lot of time for Phil, who was one of the boys, but for him to say that at that time in front of the players was out of order. Even though I'm sure he was just as gutted about having to admit it, I didn't take too kindly to it.

Thankfully, he was wrong.

Craig Levein of Hearts was out for a lengthy period with *one* damaged ligament. Ian had all but totally destroyed three out of the four. That underlines the remarkable achievement he made, and the hard work and skill of the medical people involved, in returning to the game at all, never mind at the highest level. But I always believed he'd be back. Throughout my own career people had constantly written me off because of the cartilage problems I had as a kid, even though my ops were minor compared to these. I thought, 'Give him a chance.' Everyone else seemed to be writing him off without giving him the opportunity to try a comeback. Deep down I felt he would make it because he's a tough wee cookie. Now he's showed the lot of them. Since his return he has performed unbelievably. It's tough enough just to make it back, but to do that and play at the level Ian has is fantastic.

At the time of the injury there was speculation that he could have moved abroad. He could certainly have made the grade somewhere like the Serie A, but like Coisty and a few others, he's only interested in playing for Rangers. He's been brought up with the club so all the money and glamour means nothing to him because all he wants to do is pull on a blue jersey.

Last season, when he was loaned to Everton, he was unsure about his future at Ibrox and whether he was in the manager's plans or not. But he was, he's signed a new deal and he's delighted. Guys like that love Rangers. Like Ally, he's been prepared to bide his time on the bench or on the sidelines and wait for his chance. At 28, there's still a lot of football in him. He's the type that needs regular first team football. It's seven years now since he started off on the comeback trail, but Ian still goes to the gym and does circuit training every day. He loves the Gers and loves his football and he's determined to play for as long as possible.

People are sometimes critical of testimonials which are big earners for players at clubs who are paid well over the course of their careers, but McCoist and Durrant are certainly players who deserve it. And what about the guys who move from club to club, are heroes for a couple of seasons, then go for another move to enhance career and bank balance with a big signing-on fee? Durranty and Coisty are two of a kind. They're not the highest paid players at Ibrox, but as long as they get a decent wage they're happy to turn out every week. Along with guys like Stuart McCall and Ian Ferguson, they live and breathe Rangers. They'll turn up to watch the reserves on a day off and have a good crack with the young boys at the club. A lot of senior players couldn't tell you the reserves' names.

Durranty and Ally are a great double-act when it comes to bringing younger boys out of their shell, off and on the park. And even if they couldn't kick another ball I'd have them there in the dressing-room to keep up morale.

I first came up against Durranty when I was playing in midfield for Dundee and what sticks in my mind was his great movement off the ball. I played against him just before I signed for the Gers and remember that he played a one-two with Coisty then disappeared before grabbing the goal. And ten minutes later he managed to pull off the same trick. The second was a carbon copy of the first. The wee swine had yards on you by the time you thought to wonder where he had disappeared to after making the pass.

At that time Ian would have shone even more with better players like Derek Ferguson round about him. I always got on well with him on the park and always appreciated the talent the wee man had – skills not seen in Scotland for a number of years. His passing and the runs he makes were and are fantastic. He was a legend even in his early years at Ibrox.

His first operation was in October 1988. He had another in May 1989 before testing it out when he returned to action on

February 1990 against Hearts when he led out the reserve team in front of 6,000 fans. It was discovered that one particular ligament wasn't as strong as the doctors would have liked and in April he headed to California for another op and to face his third nine-month rehabilitation period. After successful tendon replacement surgery, which wasn't available in this country, his comeback match in the reserves was against Hibernian on 19 January 1991. Needless to say, I was there.

If he didn't stand up to the rigours of playing again, that really would have been it, but he came through with flying colours. He got a tremendous boost that day to see the number of fans who'd turned up to see him. It was incredible. The whole of the Govan stand filled up and then they had to open up the Copland Road end. There were over 15,000 fans there and they were still flooding in after the game had started. It was great to see so many people turning out for one of the greats of the club. And that brings it home when you're appreciated as much. It tells you what you've done for the club when numbers like that turn up to see you on your return.

What a player he's been, and still is, for the Light Blues since he signed as a schoolboy from Glasgow United all those years ago. He's the longest serving player at the club. And he never tires of reminding Coisty, who's got the next longest service record, that he didn't have to be asked twice to sign for Rangers. That day it was really brought home to him just how much he meant to the fans. To be appreciated like that, even though he'd never admit it, gave him a big boost.

It wasn't too long after that he was back in front of a full house at Ibrox in a 0–0 draw with Hibs on 6 April 1991 when he reclaimed the number ten jersey from Mo Johnston. He went on to score his first top team goal in years in the next game against St Johnstone.

It was worth the wait, but it had been a long and difficult road back. He had a lot of battling to do and went through it most of the time with a smile on his face. To do that, with the type of injury he had suffered, speaks volumes for the wee man.

People always see the bouncy bubbly side to both Durranty and Coisty. I've seen days when Ally's been in, carrying an injury, especially when he was out for so long with his broken leg and had several aborted comebacks, and he's been told to take it easy, which is really difficult when you want to work hard to get back. All he wanted to do was drown his sorrows and have a few beers. Even when people expect you to be so up all the time, because to them you've got the lot, there are times of major depression. You can see them on a real downer, but as soon as they go out the front door and there are fans waiting for autographs and pictures, they're all smiles, willing to accommodate the club's supporters. I've seen both of them in really stinking moods and borne the brunt of it myself and, believe me, you just don't want to be around an angry McCoist or Durrant. Volatile isn't the word.

Having been in a similar situation myself with injury problems you appreciate what they are going through. And in some ways having a long term injury can help make you a better person and player. You know how much hard work and worry is involved to make it back and it stops you taking anything for granted. It makes you stronger.

In the last two years I've come back from four or five operations and my hunger for the game is stronger now than the first time I kicked a ball. That's a major factor with Durranty: every time he's been written off it makes him more determined to prove everyone wrong. I was really happy for him. He had a lot of battling to do, the majority of the time with a smile on his face, though at times I'm sure he was on a real downer. Although he's normally a bubbly character and the life and soul in the dressing-room there is another quieter side to him, which isn't seen too often. But if he didn't have that outgoing personality and sense of humour I don't think he would have got through it. Incidentally, he's the man who once came into the dressing-room on a Monday morning and told us he'd watched a great video the night before about 'these three twins'.

There were times when he really struggled to maintain his enthusiasm as he was unsettled. He was fed up and jaded before he went to Everton on loan and was unsure about whether Rangers wanted him back or not. But I went down to watch him and big Duncan Ferguson, who was loving every minute of his time on Merseyside, against Arsenal and you could see right away that Ian had reacted to the situation. He was doing things that he hadn't been doing for months at Ibrox. The change of scenery worked in his favour. That month down there he was putting in tackles, and trying his hardest to win over the fans. Dunc was enjoying himself down there too. Like Ian, he had thought he would be really upset at leaving Ibrox, but once he got a taste of being a first team hero with Everton and a really big hit with the fans there was no way he could have come back to Ibrox and gone into reserve football, with an on-form Mark Hateley keeping him out of the side.

I remember thinking that if Durranty could show Walter that type of form his worries over staying with Rangers would be over. He's said since that he really wasn't enjoying his football before that, but I don't think he's ever thought seriously about chucking it. When we came back from Everton we went to the Old Firm game at Hampden when Brian Laudrup was the hero in a 3–1 win and Ian was in among the fans with me singing his heart out, as happy as ever. And sure enough there was a new contract on the table for him. He was back in the fold.

He did go through another bad spell then, thinking, 'Rangers don't want me anymore', but that type of fear and insecurity is part of every professional footballer's life. You have to live with it. One decent pass, a good goal and you're back up there again on top of the world. That's certainly where Ian Durrant deserves to be.

Chapter Eleven

Blue Grit

I've had the privilege to have won a medal in every single one of our seven-in-a row League championship title wins in my time at Ibrox. But I'd swap the lot for the one we battled the hardest for in May 1991 and which still means more than all the others put together.

Ironically, Ian Durrant returned to the fold and scored his first goal for years in his second first team match on the comeback trail, against St Johnstone, which turned out to be Graeme Souness's last match. He finally U-turned on his decision not to take the managerial hot-seat vacated by his old pal Kenny Dalglish. Word leaked out before the announcement he wanted to make at the end of the season and he was gone, just as suddenly and amidst just as many tabloid headlines as had greeted his arrival in 1986.

We were on our own. Walter took over officially for the following game against St Mirren and after a nail-biting afternoon Sandy Robertson scored with a brave overhead kick to give us a vital two points and a winning start for Watty. It also marked my comeback after missing half a dozen matches following what proved to be a crucial last-minute defeat at Pittodrie. If we had won that, I think we would have ran away with the title as it would have been near-impossible for the Dons to catch us.

We were still in the driving seat when we beat Dundee United 1–0 at Ibrox on the Wednesday after that St Mirren game. Ian Ferguson scored with a brave diving header as he threw himself into a mêlée of boots and picked up a nasty cut in the process. That kept us two points clear, before disaster struck the following Saturday when we were gubbed 3–0 by Motherwell, to put Aberdeen on top on goal difference. Suddenly we needed a victory on the final day to clinch the title.

That was the season that relegation was scrapped halfway through and while every team was still intent on knocking us down, I felt that the Dons played sides who had the threat of relegation removed, which meant the games were virtually meaningless for them. There's a big difference playing a side who are fighting for survival and one who know their livelihoods aren't at stake and they can look forward to another season in the top flight. So they relentlessly closed the gap while we helped them out by throwing away points. The rot set in in March when we lost twice on the trot to Celtic after that defeat against the Dons, and draws against St Johnstone and Hibs in the second half of the season didn't help either.

As everyone knows, the worst day of the season was probably at Fir Park in the second last League fixture. Mark Walters missed a penalty at a crucial point in that match and we went on to lose by three goals. When we were one down we didn't realise that if it had stayed that way we would only have needed a draw to clinch the championship instead of a victory, but now a 2–1 win at Pittodrie put the Dons top on goal difference and it was they who just needed one more point to clinch it.

The atmosphere after that Motherwell mauling was certainly a sombre one, but as the week wore on, we picked ourselves back up and our confidence actually rose even though we were written off by almost everyone. One of the reasons the odds were stacked so highly against us was the ever-increasing casualty list. Like a few of the lads who played that day, there was no way I should have ever been on the pitch. The ever-worsening tendon was proving to be a real Achilles heel. On the Friday before the match I could hardly walk and I certainly couldn't jog, but I took a pain-killing injection to get me through it, trained at 3 p.m. to check the reaction and felt great.

I did the warm-up and then sat out the rest of the session beside

Walter in the Govan Stand. While the boys were having a training match he popped the million-dollar question and asked me to try and get through the game. He's not asked many players over the years to play when they're injured so there was only one answer. 'I'll be okay,' I told him. After all, I had been getting by for nearly a whole season when I'd been working in the gym for six months without kicking a ball or training with the rest of the lads. It was one of those situations, where we would have been left with Brian Reid and Scott Nisbet, who were both capable of doing a job, but lacking in the experience we needed for such a crucial match. And if we had blown it, Walter would have borne the brunt of it.

There was no way I should have been on the park, but I couldn't have lived with myself if I hadn't been there. I would always know that I would feel worse if I had cost us the championship and I wasn't there to do my bit. If you're there and you still lose you don't feel as bad.

I was fairly confident at that point that I would be able to get through the 90 minutes, but when I woke up in the hotel the next morning I panicked. The injection hadn't worn off as promised and the leg had been numb all night.

I couldn't move and I had to crawl across the floor to the toilet. A quick phone call to the Doc finally reassured me that I would be okay with another jab, but it was hardly the ideal preparation. For once, even Durranty, my room-mate, failed to see the funny side.

As the clock ticked towards 3 p.m. we were in the old players' lounge adjoining the kitchen and you could see the nerves showing on just about everybody's face. The emotion, which had built up throughout the week, was crackling in the air like electricity, although there was also a determination which had been building up as well. Then the girls in the kitchen, like Tiny, Irene and Jean and the rest, who treat us like sons, made us realise that we had to go out there fighting. One of them said: 'What a day it is for us, we're one victory away from the League title, so let's go out and do it.' That made all the boys realise that rather than contemplate the possibility of defeat we should be looking forward to a historic victory.

After needing win after win to stay with us in the title race, the Dons, for the first time in nearly two months, just needed a point and I think that proved to be their undoing. In some ways maybe it was better that we knew we had to win to make sure. The nerves were still there early in the match, but for me they were replaced by tears when Mark Hateley opened the scoring. In an unforgettable moment, Mark Walters delivered a huge cross and there was Hateley to outjump Alex McLeish and head home probably *the* most vital goal he's ever scored for Rangers.

When he arrived at the club at the start of the season, Mark took a lot of stick from the punters. He was still recovering from an ankle injury that had given him problems at Monaco, and then he and Mo formed the regular striking partnership which relegated Ally, who was the fans' favourite, to a place on the bench. But I remember him saying in the dressing-room very early on: 'Let them criticise me if they want. They pay their money and they've got every right to get on my back, but I'll win them over.' Well, that day his prediction came true. He had done well for us earlier in the season, but that afternoon's work rubber-stamped his hero status with the fans. His second goal was greeted by just as big a roar as the first and even though we'd thrown away a two-goal lead against the Dons earlier in the season, this time I was sure we wouldn't let that happen.

When the first went in I've never felt the tears come so quickly and I thought 'Get a grip of yourself', as our fans went berserk all round the stadium. The Dons had a couple of chances early on and if they had scored our task would have been phenomenal. But Woodsy did a great job and thankfully was on hand to make some good saves.

I had a second injection to help keep me going, but not long after the break I felt as if I'd been shot by a sniper in the stands. As I collapsed to the turf in agony my first thought was that I had torn a calf muscle, though I later discovered that the tendon had ruptured. Gordon Allison, who was our physiotherapist at the time, ran on with the wet sponge, but I immediately demanded a stretcher knowing there was no way I could carry on.

At that point Mark Walters ran over shouting, 'Gordon, Gordon . . . my hamstring's a bit tight, I think I'll have to come off.' My response was unprintable as I pointed out that, unlike him, I actually had an injury, and a pretty painful one at that. The agony didn't end there as I had to listen to the oohs and aahs of the crowd from a small room just off the tunnel as we battled our way towards the final whistle and the final roar of acknowledgment when we clinched the title.

I demanded some help from a security guard, who returned with an antique wheelchair that was lying around the stadium before being dispatched again with orders to find crutches from somewhere. I was desperate to get back out there and join the celebrations, but first I headed for the dressing-room, the away one which we were using because of the reconstruction work at Ibrox at the time. A lot of the boys were really emotional there, and then we took the field again for some great celebrations as stand-in skipper Nigel Spackman lifted the League Championship trophy.

By the end of the match, it really was a case of the walking wounded. McCoist and Durrant, who had only just returned to first team action, weren't fully fit and there were another half a dozen guys who under normal circumstances would have been rested. Then, of course, we were missing skipper Richard Gough, who listened to the match from his hospital bed. And not long into the match we suffered another blow when Tom Cowan broke his leg in a clash with Hans Gillhaus.

After I retired we had guys like Terry Hurlock, Nigel Spackman, Mark Hateley and even McCoist playing in defence. For the record, the team that day was: Woods, Stevens, Cowan, Nisbet, Spackman, Brown, Hurlock, Ferguson, Hateley, Johnston, Walters with Durrant and McCoist on the bench.

I think the majority of them would agree that win was simply the best. Completing the treble a few years after that was special, but the heart and guts that we found to produce that result were very special. Defeat that day, even now, doesn't bear thinking about. We would never have lived it down and although we would probably have got on with it, and perhaps went on to win other trophies, we would always have been known as the Rangers team who blew the championship, in the same way as the Hearts team of 1986 aren't allowed to forget that they came so close to the Double and lost the lot. We would have been sick for a long time afterwards if we had blown that, but on the big occasion we answered the call and proved we won't take second best. Look at Aberdeen and all the other second prizes they've won since.

The party that night was tremendous. Graeme Clark and a few of the Wet, Wet, Wet lads were there as the champagne flowed in the players lounge and the celebrations kicked off. Later, Coisty and I and Allison and Diana ended up in East Kilbride and Ally and I sat up to seven in the morning, just reliving every moment of what had been a wonderful day. The next day I went to see Goughie in Ross Hall hospital even though the Doc had said not to bother, because I knew for a fact that, had the roles been reversed, I would have liked someone to visit me if I had missed out through illness.

It was important for the manager and Archie to get their partnership off to a flyer and Walter was absolutely delighted. Afterwards he told me just to go out and enjoy my summer. And having a full-length plaster on didn't stop me having the biggest party ever for two months. When we came back in August the Gaffer asked me what I'd been up to and I told him straight that I had been an absolute disgrace for the entire close season. 'Good. That's how it should have been,' he replied. It was nice to know that Walter knew you'd done your best for him and he was prepared to let you enjoy the success.

Looking back on that season, which was the most eventful yet for a variety of reasons, I realise just what a great achievement it was. For a kick-off, the top deck of the Main Stand was being built in the first half of the season and that meant a terrific upheaval for everyone. We spent much of it getting changed at the Strathclyde Police sports club at Lochinch, next to Haggs Castle golf club about a mile from Ibrox, and either training there or some other ground. There was a temporary gym set up along with the coaching staff's offices and players' kitchen over in the Govan

Stand. And I was to spend a lot of time there with Graeme Souness giving me circuits to do as I couldn't train properly. It doesn't sound too great a hardship, but we were out of our own environment, the one we had been used to for years and believe me, it did have an affect. None of that worked in our favour. During the period we were changing at Lochinch, a lot of the lads wouldn't even bother going into Ibrox for lunch and just head straight for home instead. The girls in the kitchen missed us because they might not see us from Saturday to Saturday in some cases.

Everything seemed to be against us until we finally managed to pull it off on that last great day. By the time the season finished we had a new-look stadium, a new captain, a new manager and a new League set-up! But one thing remained constant. The sheer will to win and battling qualities that have been the hallmark of great Rangers teams throughout the years that took us to a hat-trick of titles.

Chapter Twelve

The Gaffers

The biggest betting coup at Ibrox in recent years has to have been when Walter took over as boss. The lads were told a few days before the news was released officially and at that time a number of other names were being tipped for the job. In reality, Walter had been offered it almost immediately after Graeme's departure. And we took full advantage. I had a few people out laying discreet bets around the place and made a tidy sum. I took some revenge on the bookies for once.

To be the ninth manager of Rangers Football Club is a huge job, but I think Walter Smith has handled it brilliantly. Graeme may have helped show him a few things in his time there, but all Walter's years at Dundee United as a player and coach have helped him learn the trade. People always ask what he's like – level-headed is probably the best description. The advice he gives is always sound and he's approachable. But in other ways, he can be just as hard as Graeme and neither of them suffer fools gladly.

I was disappointed when he left me out of the AEK Athens game last season, but when I thought about it he was probably right. I was getting by, but I wasn't in top form and I wasn't playing the way I had two seasons before. I didn't have that buzz you get when you're injury free and the Gaffer had spotted that and made the correct decision. It's a hard job, but when he's made tough decisions, nine out of ten are right, although he would admit to mistakes.

Since the Treble season, when we've lost it's because key players have been injured and performances haven't come, not through any of the manager's doing. The only time I've seen Walter really lose it was on the bus home from Tannadice when we captured the League title there in 1989. During the high jinks on the bus down the road I emptied a bucket of champagne with the iced water in it over him. Unfortunately, the bucket caught him and cut his head and the fact that he was dressed to go out that night with his wife, Ethel, obviously didn't help either.

'You! Ya b------,' he roared. 'You're lucky to be here. I'm going to sell you to Stranraer first thing on Monday morning.'

If you're not happy or have problems off or on the park you can go to him. All you have to do is pick up the phone – he's better than the Samaritans. If players work hard for him, he'll push himself to make sure everyone's happy. You get the odd player who gets fed up if he's been left out of the side. But he's dropped me too and I don't have a bad word to say about him. He's always treated me fairly and if he does drop you it's for a good reason and he'll take you aside and explain it. I'll usually know if I'm not playing as well as I should be but other players can't accept that and that's when problems begin.

Walter, his wife Ethel and their two boys are all down to earth. He'll have a pint with the lads on occasions and never forgets where he's come from. Graeme could be just as good company when he wanted to be, but he tended to distance himself a bit more, leaving Walter to have the most contact with the squad.

When Walter first took over as manager, there were plenty of pundits eager to point out that he would find it harder than Graeme, who was a bigger name, to bring top-class players to Ibrox. Well, they've certainly been proved wrong on that one. It's another feather in his cap that he's managed to sign Paul Gascoigne in the face of stiff competion from other clubs. But Gazza had met Walter on holiday beforehand and they got on well together and I think he'll have the same respect and bond with him as he did with Terry Venables earlier in his career.

When Walter took over, no matter what doubts fans or the press may have had, there was never any doubt in the players' minds that he was the best man for the job. He had the respect of everyone at Ibrox and as far as we were concerned we were all desperate to carry on and win the League title for him. Although he's always quick to give Graeme credit for that season, there's no doubt that it took an extra special performance to grab the title back on the last day of the season.

Walter has gone on to be one of the most successful managers the club has ever had. No one else has won the eight trophies he has in the last four years or been so close to back-to-back Trebles. He was not given the credit he was due for his tactics in Europe in the season we were unbeaten in the Champions League and the earlier rounds. And yet, so high are the standards that he's helped set that two defeats in a row is enough to spark an 'Ibrox crisis' and draw question marks over his future. That's obviously ridiculous, because his record speaks for itself. But it's part and parcel of having the most demanding and high pressure job in Scottish football.

In recent seasons, after early exits in Europe, he has taken a lot of stick from some sections of the support who, to me, aren't really Rangers fans. They're out there demanding changes at the top left, right and centre, but have no real answers themselves. Walter is the best man for the job, simply because no one else could do it better. His biggest problem is that once he's signed what he hopes are three world-class foreign players for Europe, he's then got to choose from the best in Scotland and I think it's generally agreed that the reservoir of genuinely world-class talent is drying up season by season. Another problem facing Walter in the seasons ahead will be replacing guys like McCoist, Durrant, Ferguson and Gough, who know what it means to play for the jersey and push themselves that wee bit harder to meet the demands of playing at Ibrox.

German or Italian clubs, for example, have a much larger population and therefore more players to choose from. They also have far greater financial resources. Our fans weren't delighted about forking out £30 a time for a ticket for this season's Champions League matches, but as the supporters who went to our game against Juventus in Turin found out, the tickets were three times the price. Consequently, even though what we spend on players is big money in Scottish terms, it's probably average for the big clubs in England and peanuts compared to what Milan or Juventus can afford.

Another big problem is that when you do sign big stars, no matter how good they are, they need time to fit in with the team and for the side to gel, and that's time that we haven't had in recent seasons as the first hurdle in Europe has come even before we're under starter's orders in the Premier League.

Even though the Gaffer isn't one to make excuses, I feel some sections of the support fail to understand that sometimes players are out there when they're less than 100 per cent fit. And although I accept that the team has to be performing well to get the fans excited, they also fail to realise just how much of a lift their backing can give players rather than negative barracking. Since Ibrox has become all-seated the atmosphere has suffered and that's something we've got to get back.

Walter handles himself a lot better in terms of dealing with the media and has adopted a much lower profile than Graeme found it possible to do, partly because of his own nature, partly because of the hype surrounding the club in his time here and the combatative and uncompromising attitude he had on the pitch as well. Both are similar in their desire to protect their players wherever possible. Neither will criticise players in public and whatever is said in the dressing-room after a defeat stays there. They both would always accept responsibility. Walter will never blame referees or his players for a defeat and even though he's a Rangers man through and through, and has stood on the terraces at Ibrox, he'll be just as cut up inside, although he won't show it.

However, Walter is more approachable than Graeme Souness was and always explains his decisions to you. And even though he and Archie tend to let us enjoy ourselves and blow off a bit of steam, particulary when we're doing well, you always know who's boss and neither of them are guys you want to push too far.

He was in the perfect position to take over after being Graeme's right-hand man since 1986. He's now built up a good partnership with the chairman, David Murray, who has done wonders for the club since he took control from the Lawrence Group in 1988. His business skills have made him a man everyone respects. And even though the Souness revolution had a huge impact at Ibrox, and in Scottish football in general, people are quick to forget what his arrival from Sampdoria did for the club.

One of my first dealings with Souness came in 1986. The day after we beat Hearts to end their title dreams at Dens, I travelled to Glasgow with Robert Connor to take part in a testimonial match for Kenny Dalglish at Hampden. The Celtic lads made us welcome that afternoon when we met up at the hotel before the match, as our win over Hearts had handed them the title. But equally welcoming were Souness and guys like Alan Hansen, whom I ended up sitting at the same table with over lunch.

I was on the bench for that game and with 35 minutes to go Tommy Docherty, the boss of our select side, turned to me and said: 'Son, where do you play?'

'Middle of the park.'

'Right then, I'm taking Frank Gray off and I want you to go into the middle and tell Souness to move over to the right side.'

'It's okay, I'll play on the right, I don't mind,' I said quickly.

'Naw, son, you go out there and enjoy yourself.'

I thought, I can't say that to Graeme Souness, the man's a legend and here's John Brown from Dundee taking over, but I ran on to the park and said, 'Graeme, the Doc says do you mind moving over a wee bit?' And he went and let me take over his position. Needless to say, I thoroughly enjoyed the experience, being on the same pitch as guys like him and Dalglish.

I had a lot of time for Graeme. He brought me to Rangers and he was one of the most talented Scottish players ever. You just look at his European Cup and Championship medals with Liverpool, and his Scottish caps. Working with him and playing alongside him was a great honour. With that inbuilt self-confidence or arrogance, depending on how you looked at it, he started to upset some people. However, whenever he took us out for lunch or you saw him with his family he was a different guy. Walter got the press back on our side after Graeme had alienated himself with certain people, though no doubt some of them deserved it.

When Graeme moved to Liverpool I think it was a case of the heart ruling the head. When you're as wealthy as he is the money doesn't come into it. For all players, your playing days are the best of your life and the best time he ever had was playing for Liverpool at their peak, especially in those three memorable European Cup finals. I think the memory of those times and the chance to take them back to that level swayed his decision. At Ibrox the only real challenge left was in Europe and Graeme always loved a challenge and the chance to put one over on people who didn't think he could do it. I think at first he turned down Liverpool's approach, but in the end he wasn't able to resist the lure of going back to his first love. When we played against St Johnstone in the 3-0 game his team talk centred around the virtues of being committed to the club and loyalty, pointing out that unless you were there was no place for you at Ibrox. Two days later he was gone, which after that Saturday's team talk I couldn't believe. But you have to accept that you're in a game which is professional, people have to do things for their own benefit. He gave a lot to Rangers and worked round the clock for them so I don't think anyone can hold it against him that he did go. The timing could certainly have been better, but I don't think that was of his choosing. He wanted to see out the season with us, before moving on, but the news leaked out and David Murray moved quickly to end any doubts. You couldn't have a manager who was unsettled with so many big games to play.

The chairman said at the time that he thought it was the biggest mistake Graeme had ever made and sadly he was proved to be correct.

After Walter took over and we did eventually clinch the title, being the type of guy he is he was quick to pay tribute to Graeme's contribution, in building up the team and leading us for over 30 games that year. Sadly, it didn't work out for him back at Anfield, but I hope he's still enjoying his football in Turkey.

The most controversial incidents in Graeme's time were, of course, the fall-outs with Graham Roberts, Terry Butcher and Mo

Johnston when he arrived home early from Italy after a pre-season bust-up.

During the Roberts affair, I was in the sauna and missed most of the action, although I know that even though the usual rumours were flying about dressing-room punch-ups, that wasn't the case. There was a heated 'discussion' before Roberts overstepped the mark and was told he would be sold. He then spent a brief period in the reserves and the press had a field day when he was banished to the Highlands where the second string had a couple of matches. This was regarded as petty and designed to humiliate him, but as far as Graeme was concerned, he had to show his authority, that he was the boss and he didn't want someone who could have been a disruptive influence around the first team squad. This upset a few fans, who rightly regarded Robbo as a hero for what he'd done for the club since arriving from Spurs, but it was nothing compared to the flak that the manager took in the wake of Terry Butcher's departure.

Leaving the captain out of the League Cup final and his subsequent transfer caused a lot of upheaval at the time. But there's two sides to every story and Graeme would later claim that Terry's fitness and failure to go for an operation the previous summer were the main factors in ending his Ibrox career, though at the time he didn't expand on what had happened, and when Terry didn't start shooting his mouth off after he'd moved on, the matter was closed. But at the time, just as with the Roberts incident, the manager was portrayed as the villain of the piece and there's no doubt the fans were right behind big Butch. The actual discussion the two of them had before Terry was left out of that semi-final, is something that remains between them.

I took over from Oleg Kuznetsov for our match with Red Star Belgrade, in Yugoslavia, and we found ourselves all but out after that first leg when we lost 3–0, with yours truly scoring an own goal. I took pelters for my performance and I'll never forget hearing that Derek Johnstone had said on the radio that a half-fit Terry Butcher would have done a better job than I did, which really hurt. The second leg wasn't much fun either. I had been out of the side for a couple of weeks, having been dropped to make room for Oleg Kuznetsov, even though I had initially taken over the number six jersey filled by Butch, so I was a yard or two short, particularly for the pace the European game is played at.

The following Sunday, when we faced Celtic in the Skol Cup final at Hampden, I had a real point to prove and fortunately we turned things around and recorded a fine extra-time victory. After Paul Elliot had opened the scoring for Celtic we hit back, with Mark Walters equalising and Richard Gough grabbing the all-important winner to get his captaincy off to a winning start. It was great to get a result like that after the disappointment of Europe and being written off. On a personal level, I felt I had answered some of the criticism I had taken against Red Star four days previously. We were under a lot of pressure, but sometimes that works in your favour.

After that, following Terry's bust up, it was just a matter of time before he moved and he signed for Coventry City as player/manager. Rangers did well to get the money they did for him, which was only £150,000 less than Souness had paid Ipswich in 1986. The doubts over his fitness were proved to be well founded when his knee forced him to give up playing not too long afterwards.

It was sad to see Terry go under such circumstances. I was a big fan of his off and on the park. He was a great leader and captain, a world-class player, and a great ambassador for the club. He really took Rangers and the fans to his heart and vice versa. It was a rough spell for him, but I think it backfired on him when he went with England to Italia '90 against Souness's wishes and put country before club. You could understand perfectly why he did that though: it was his last chance to play at the very highest level in a World Cup and he was prepared to take the risk with his knee.

It wasn't generally known at the time, but a few people were aware of the situation, and when we lost out in Europe and Terry said he wasn't fit for the Skol Cup semi-final against Aberdeen, it all came to a head.

He gave great service to Rangers in his time. The fans loved him and he still loves the club. It's hard for anyone to leave Ibrox and not be affected by the place and the people, they have so many happy memories to take with them.

Another headline grabber for Souness was his fall-out with Mo Johnston at our pre-season training camp in Italy, when it was said that the disagreement ended with a punch-up. Even though the rumours about the 'true' story circulated for months, the official version was the correct one. We were more than halfway through our by then traditional week-long stint high in the Tuscany hills at the Il Ciocco hotel and sports complex. The boys had been given permission to have a few beers and although some maybe reinterpreted the rules and had a fairly loose concept of 'a few', no one had gone over the top. We had been through a hard week with twice-daily training sessions in heat and at altitude and in those conditions even a couple of pints is enough to have an effect and promote a few high jinks.

Scott Nisbet, as he always did, had removed his mattress from the bed and was sleeping on the floor when a merry Mo appeared in his room in the early hours.

Scott just had time to say 'Who is it?' from the floor before Mo dived across the pitch black room which had the shutters closed and landed head first on a bed of springs instead of a sleeping Nissy, who was in hysterics as he heard the anguished and muffled swearing from the other side of the room.

That was it. Proof that truth is stranger than fiction sometimes. Of course, according to the unofficial versions either myself, Fergie or Graeme had hooked him and were responsible for the cut and battered state of his coupon. Even now people still prefer to believe the version they heard as gospel from Ally McCoist's second cousin twice-removed's next door neighbour.

The next day Mo was actually sitting next to me at the team meeting until myself and Stuart Munro demanded that he find another seat so we wouldn't be in the firing line if the expected fireworks started.

We had the meeting and it was a relatively calm affair. Souness wanted Mo to apologise and Mo being Mo wouldn't. His attitude was 'I give you 100 per cent on the park and what I do in my own time is my business', which I think he was wrong about. Souness gave him a chance to say sorry, he didn't take it and he was on the next plane home. Now, whether flying home was the Gaffer's idea or Mo's, I don't know. We were told to get on the bus to take us to the training ground and when we returned he was gone. Whether more words were exchanged and Mo upped and left or whether Graeme ordered him home is anybody's guess. The outcome was the same.

When the first pictures of his battle-scarred and scratched face were published, the press had a field day and as far as they were concerned Mo was finished at Ibrox. But eventually he cooled down when he was back at Ibrox and did what he should have done all along – apologised to the manager. The incident was then forgotten. Mo went on to score more goals for us before following Graeme to Merseyside when he was no longer guaranteed a first team place as Coisty and Mark Hateley became the dominant partnership.

Of course, Maurice was always going to be the centre of attention no matter what he did at Ibrox after his shock signing in July 1989. Coisty was the only one who had an inkling of what was in the air as we headed off to Italy and found out that the wee man was to be our first major Catholic signing. Of course, the fact that he had recently declared himself ready for a second spell at Parkhead days before the 1989 Scottish Cup final only added to the controversy.

We were in the dressing-room after that game, having lost 1–0, when Souness stormed in. The first thing he did was throw his runners-up medal into the bath. 'That's no good to me,' he stormed. 'I'm only interested in winners' medals.' Then later he seemed pretty chuffed when he told us: 'Never mind, we're going to do something which will knock them for six.'

Of course, at the time, nobody had any idea what his plans were and it was only when we were in Ciocco that the penny dropped. The following day Mo arrived in the helicopter (or gunship as we nicknamed it) that had flown him from Pisa airport with his agent Bill McMurdo. Understandably, he looked a bag of nerves and he was immediately the target for some good-natured abuse.

Our kit man, Jimmy Bell, used to come round the rooms and dish out chocolate and sweeties to the players, but there are no prizes for guessing who was a Mars bar short when he arrived at the McCoist and Johnston residence at the end of the corridor. And on his first day we set up a table with bread and water while we all sat together tucking into pasta. Derek Ferguson, with tongue firmly in his cheek, also delared at training when we heard the news that we were now 'a non-secretarial' club.

But Mo was to win everyone over. His last-minute winner against Celtic in November 1989 convinced the vast majority of the support that he could do a good job for us and he really did give his all. A lot of people had their own opinions, but during his time at the club he never let down the team and scored some crucial goals, particularly in that first season.

Souness hit the headlines over the years in a number of stories that had absolutely nothing to do with football. For example, his supposed fall-out with some tea-lady at St Johnstone was blown out of all proportion. And he wasn't the only one to attract unwanted attention at McDiarmid Park. Walter and the Saints boss at that time, Alex Totten, both found themselves in court after a well-publicised bust-up in the tunnel. In my view the police over-reacted to the situation. It had a funny side as well, and a not so happy ending for first team coach Davie Dodds. The court case came during our end of season trip to Monaco and because, along with Archie Knox, he was one of the witnesses, Doddsy wasn't able to come and keep an eye on us. John McGregor and Billy Kirkwood took his place, but what made matters even worse was the fact that Davie wasn't even called. He's never forgiven the Gaffer for that one, but along with the rest of the lads he enjoyed a recent training session when Walter played himself in one of the kickabouts and fell flat on his face as he tried to trap a ball (sorry, Walter). It was the funniest sight for a long time.

Going back to storms in a teacup, yes, Graeme may have had the odd argument with the Ibrox crockery, but it was always as a result of sheer frustration because of the high standards he set for himself and for the club. He wanted the team to play the way he did: put on a show, throw in a bit of arrogance and win games in style. He was a perfectionist and you could understand why he got upset when players didn't listen to what he had told them.

But he was a winner. Second prizes weren't good enough and that was a great attitude to have and one which rubbed off on the rest of us.

On one occasion he got the blame for having a smashing time in the away team's dressing-room at East End Park when we lost out to Dunfermline in the Scottish Cup. But I have to confess that it was me. When I was sent off just before half-time, I was in tears and let fly in a moment of anger and frustration as I came in. Souness had a few words of comfort for me and even a wee kiss on the top of the head — I don't know who that was a worse experience for. I was still gutted after it and Terry Butcher, who was injured, came down from the stand and sat with me in the dressing-room for the rest of the game.

I haven't got a bad word to say about Graeme. I don't know if he was appreciated the way he should have been in Scotland. He had an arrogant streak, but he knew what he wanted and was a winner. At times you felt hard done by over some of the things he would say to you but it was important that you didn't take it to heart and realised that he was digging you up for a reason. Different players reacted in different ways, but there were no real winners in arguments with Graeme. He was the boss, and that was all there was to it. It wasn't open for discussion.

Personally, he signed me and he stuck by me. If you gave him 100 per cent he'd give you the same plus interest back. He had his volatile moments, but sometimes we deserved them. He was such a perfectionist. If you didn't turn on a five-star show he was angry.

Graeme did take things to heart, especially some of the treatment he was handed out by the press. His reaction was usually a ban or another bust-up which maybe wasn't the right way to handle the situation. He always wanted us to stick together. There was a kind of siege mentality. It was us against the world, which wasn't that far from the truth. People were always waiting in the wings ready to have a pop at us and he had us believing that success and strength came through working hard for each other and stuff anyone outside the club.

I've played under managers who could really shoot you down in flames at half-time or after a game. But with Graeme, the criticism was nearly always constructive, rather than just bawling you out.

It's not just me who's got plenty to thank him for. Before Souness what was the average wage, even for top players in Scotland, and what did a successful Rangers do to raise attendances at every other ground in the country they played at? He changed the trend of top stars having to move south to earn a decent living and his name alone was enough to attract the big names in England for the first time. Before his arrival even guys like Davie Cooper and Coisty, international players, would have been on a pittance compared to their English counterparts.

He built up Rangers to such an extent that when Walter took over the club's name was enough to attract the top stars. And since Walter led us to the Treble and our last Champions League run, the club's profile has increased throughout Europe. But without Graeme being brought from Genoa to Govan by former chairman David Holmes none of it would have happened. David Murray would probably never have been involved with the club. Walter could be with another Scottish side and who knows what kind of state the game in this country would be in without his impact on the whole scene?

Chapter Thirteen

Scots On The Rox

Playing for your country is the ambition of just about everyone who's ever pulled on a pair of boots. And I was no different. But after a long spell of being just about the only player in the Ibrox dressing-room without a cap, when my chance to become an internationalist finally came about I turned it down. That might seem crazy, but I had my reasons.

The press had mentioned my name on more than a couple of occasions because of my club form, in the Premier and Champions Leagues, and a few of our players had also remarked that it was ridiculous that I wasn't even in the squad. But I was having such a good time with Rangers during that first Champions League season that it didn't bother me too much. Eventually, though, I got a call one Friday afternoon on the golf course, after a few call-offs to the squad for our match with Portugal at home.

I should have known then really that I was never destined to wear the dark blue. I called Andy and got his wife who told me he was out. 'Can you tell him John Brown called?'

'Which newspaper are you from?' she asked, underlining the fact that I wasn't a player Andy had been raving about.

Finally, when I spoke to Andy himself he said: 'I'm pulling you into the squad. Come along and enjoy a few days with us. You'll really enjoy it.'

After being involved at the top level with Rangers either in the starting line-up or on the bench it's a strange feeling to get to that age at the peak of you career and find you're not a part of the

131

manager's plans, even if technically you're in the squad. It was also a weird feeling to walk into the dressing-room at Ibrox, which was full of unfamiliar faces, and have McCoist ask you what you think you're doing there.

I went up to Dunkeld House in Perth where the squad were staying and the highlight for me had to be going fishing with McCoist and Durrant. There was clay pigeon shooting and golf on the agenda as well, but the fishing was a hoot. We were absolutely knackered after being in the water for about eight hours. The stretch of river we were on must have cost a fortune to fish, but one poor guy certainly didn't get his money's worth as he spent the entire day putting a new hook or fly on Ally's line. His casting was wild and I think he caught just about everything apart from a fish.

I was rooming with Ian Ferguson as usual. He had spent the day clay pigeon shooting, though he came close to turning the gun on Hearts John Robertson, who's another good lad but was talking 19 to the dozen and putting Fergie off. I knew a few guys, like Gary McAllister of Leeds and boys from other Premier Division clubs, but I have to say I didn't really feel a part of it. I felt as though I was just there to keep the press happy. They were the ones who had been calling for my inclusion.

At training, Roxburgh was going with three at the back and getting them working together with the full-backs, and again I didn't feel comfortable. I was quite glad in the end to get away.

I sat on the bench when we drew 0–0 with Portugal. Then for the friendly with Germany which followed Andy stated that he wanted to use youth for the game, so I was out in the cold again. It didn't help when the 'youth policy' involved bringing in guys even *older* than me. I must admit I was really disappointed, because I had never played for my country and I thought a friendly on home turf would have been the ideal place to give me a chance to show what I could do, especially as I might have been needed for the away match with Portugal in the World Cup qualifier. But not meeting the age requirement, I was never considered.

The crunch came on an emotional night when we played CSKA Moscow in the final match of our Champions League section and narrowly lost out on a place in the European Cup final.

I was in a group of around 30 who were being considered for a place in the Scotland squad for the Portugal match which was being named the next day.

After the CSKA match, like other club doctors, ours had to tell the SFA whether or not I could be considered and, even though I was fit, I told him to tell Andy Roxburgh, who was in the manager's office, having watched our match, that I wasn't available and not to consider me. Two minutes later, Archie came along to the treament room and told me: 'Don't be daft, just go.' But I had made up my mind and that was it, whether it ruled out any further chances with Scotland or not.

It might seem crazy, particularly as a few of the Scotland defenders were doubtful and I could have been in contention, but I felt totally drained that night after our European efforts and I was upset at us failing at the final hurdle.

Now we were out of that I thought, 'We've got a Treble to go for,' and I wanted to be 100 per cent for that. Rangers mean more to me and my loyalties are with the club and to Walter and Archie, who had stuck with me in the past, not to Andy Roxburgh who had never done me any favours. I wanted to make sure I was okay for the run-in to the title.

If I had been quoted by Scotland and had at least been given the chance I thought I had earned to show what I could do at international level, I might have had a different perspective and gone out and given my all for Scotland. Having seen some of the players who were picked over the years, I know that I was at least worth a try-out. But I had never been given that opportunity and the club came first.

I'm not trying to be smug, as I'm as desperate for Scotland to do well as the next man, but that Portugal game turned out to be a disaster and I was glad I wasn't there. We lost 5–0 and Coisty paid a terrible price, breaking his leg and missing the run-in to the Treble-winning season.

The team, particularly the defence, was slaughtered for the display, which wasn't really fair. Stewart McKimmie, the Aberdeen full-back, had been out for virtually six months beforehand and Jim McInally of Dundee United, and now Raith Rovers, hadn't played in the five weeks between the German match and the Portugal trip. There are no guarantees, but I felt as though I could have done a job there. Roxburgh was always quoted as saying 'We've got plenty of cover for defence', but in the end did they qualify for the World Cup?

My original impression of him was backed up when he let the players take the flak for that defeat and it was that which led to his infamous bust-up with Richard Gough on the way back. Roxburgh body-swerved his responsibility. There were guys out there trying to do a job for him in an important World Cup qualifier and they bore the brunt of the criticism while the manager got off lightly. To me a good manager will take the flak away from players in public, even if he personally has destroyed each and every one of them in the dressing-room after the game.

Another point I would like to make is that during that season, whether or not I merited a place or not, the Rangers defence was immense and every one of the rest of our lads, including our goalkeeper, played for their country.

But what surprised me that season was that they persisted with the usual midfield. I don't think on the form they were showing, and the partnership they had forged in midfield, you could afford to leave out Stuart McCall or Ian Ferguson. You're probably thinking, why doesn't he go one step further and just name the entire Rangers team? Well, for one, some of them aren't Scottish, although Nigel MacSpackman wasn't exactly the real McCoy and nearly made it. Spacks was a team-mate and a good player, but when you're a real Scot and you're desperate to play and you see the manager trying to bring in someone who's been to Burntisland once, it makes a mockery of the system, no matter how much you want to win.

But if we're talking Scots here, I seriously don't see why the players involved have to be spread from clubs up and down the League table and not just the most successful ones. It stands to reason that your biggest clubs should always be providing the bulk of the players as they are the ones who can afford to buy the best in the country. I reckon that sometimes you have a situation where the national coach is trying to satisfy all the clubs by sprinkling a couple of players from each, which I think is a nonsense. What you needed was a manager who had the balls to say, 'Stuff everyone else, I'm going to do my own thing.' I don't think Roxburgh was that man.

There's no doubt it's a tough job, but I think Craig Brown has done well since he took over. I must admit that, like a few people at the time, I thought we needed a big name who would have helped get everyone behind the team again, but Craig looks as if he's taking us to the European Championships in 1996, so you cannot fault the job he's done with the players he has had available to him.

One thing I would criticise him for is not recalling Richard Gough to the squad. It still surprises me that a small nation like Scotland can afford to do without his services. He leads by example and is a dominating character. On form he's hard to beat. It's quite ironic that he's in the SFA Hall of Fame, having made over 50 appearances for his country and yet now he's still out in the cold after that fall-out with Andy Roxburgh.

Okay, Craig was Andy's assistant at that time, but if you look around other countries in Europe, players and national bosses don't always see eye to eye: that doesn't stop them putting aside their differences for the good of the team. Fair enough if Richard was past it, but he is still one of the fittest guys at Ibrox. He's a true professional in the way he looks after himself and, as he proved in the Old Firm victory in the Coca-Cola Cup quarter-final at Parkhead earlier this season, he's on superb form.

Apart from that, like everyone else, I hope the fans get right behind Craig Brown and the team and get the passion back. Oh, and if you're reading this, Craig, I can get you our reserve fixture list if you want a thirty-something look to the team.

Looking back on all the success and medals I've enjoyed with Rangers, a cap would have been nice to add to the collection. It's a big regret for me, not playing for Scotland, but I look at some of the people who have been capped and you realise if they give out caps that cheaply, maybe I'm better off without one.

Chapter Fourteen

Final Countdown

The toughest decision I've ever had to make in my Ibrox career came in the 1993/94 season as we set our sights on what could have been a historic second consecutive Treble-winning season. And the player who helped make up my mind for me was Dundee United's pacy winger Jerren Nixon.

Having already claimed the League Cup after an extra-time win over Hibs at Parkhead, the League Championship was also on the cards and we were through to the Scottish Cup final against Dundee United. I had struggled with a recurring groin injury throughout the season and a crucial few seconds in our last League fixture against United on 23 April totally destroyed me and caused me to make the heart-breaking decision that would eventually cost me a place in the Cup final team.

We beat United 2–1 that day, but when Nixon ran right past me and crossed for the opening goal, I knew it was time to bring the curtain down on my season. I was totally embarrassed at the way he sprinted past me without me getting a challenge in. And even though a few of the lads pointed out that he was so fast he could do that to anyone on his day, I felt a right clown and I knew it was time to chuck it and have an operation to end my problems. Without making excuses, my groin had really bothered me throughout the season. Normally I might have tried to carry on, resting it wherever possible and try and make it through to the last game in May, but the showing up I got that day convinced me I had done as much as I could in that campaign, even although it wasn't the sole factor in my decision.

137

There's nothing worse for any player than when you're unable to train and you're just turning out for games and struggling to get through. The pain barrier I was constantly trying to break through played a major part in my thinking.

After watching the horror story on the telly and being really tormented by it, I spoke to the manager a couple of days later. He told me to forget the incident and pointed out that I had done well after that and helped push us towards our eventual 2–1 victory. He wanted me to leave it for a couple of weeks to see if it settled down. But I knew if I left it until after the Cup final I would then be struggling again to get my fitness back at the start of the following season.

I also felt we had enough depth in the squad to win in the final, but having already missed out on the League Cup final earlier in the season, it was a really hard decision to take and the thought of being there if we clinched another Treble was certainly a tempting one.

Normally I would have agreed to try a rest cure, especially after the drama of that 1991 title win where a similar approach meant I could take my place in the starting line-up, even if I didn't last the full 90 minutes. But this time round I couldn't kid myself on. It felt so bad I knew I wasn't going to be right mentally or physically and I didn't think I could do myself or the team justice.

I wasn't the only one suffering. After the hard work of that 1992/93 season, the team which had played together for 18 months and brought the club so much success was effectively broken up as around 11 of that squad were recovering from ops and not firing on all cylinders as a result. Although the fans sometimes don't realise it, a lot of players in that season in particular were turning out less than 100 per cent fit and not at their peak, and that has a dramatic effect on the team's performances. We were missing essential personnel who had played a crucial part in our earlier successes, like Ally McCoist and Andy Goram. Coisty only played 19 games that term and Andy came in late in the season after recovering from his knee operation. He made his first appearance of the season against Hibs in February, but played just ten games before missing the rest of the season after collapsing with a thigh injury at Tannadice.

I was in and out of hospital and ended up having a string of operations within the space of 18 months. Before my first groin operation I had a routine where I would play the 90 minutes and get through the game, but my muscles would stiffen up later and it would take three or four days to settle down. I started off not doing much training at all and eventually I was doing nothing from Saturday to Saturday. It was real torture. The Doc gave me a finger check at one point and I hit the roof with the pain.

After scoring in the quarter-final of the Scottish Cup against Hearts at Ibrox, I played in the first Hampden semi-final against Kilmarnock. But I was gutted for a week to be dropped for the replay, which we eventually won thanks to a controversial Mark Hateley goal, with Killie players insisting the ball hadn't crossed the line. I was out because the manager reckoned I wouldn't be able to cope with playing Saturday and Wednesday and brought in Steven Pressley even though I was raring to go.

The season had got off to a bad start when our European bubble burst and our run came to an end in Sofia. That game, like the other qualifying rounds which were to follow, really came too early. But we were still just seconds from making the Champions League again when Nikolai Todorov found the top corner of the net from just over the halfway line in the second leg. A Dave McPherson strike and a double from Mark Hateley gave us a 3–2 win at Ibrox in the first leg and Ian Durrant's goal in the return leg seemed to be enough to take us through, until that last-minute heartbreaker when a split second of slackness put the Bulgarians through on the away goals rule after a 4–4 aggregate score.

It was a dismal start to the season and my own fortunes were to mirror the team's. After just two games against Hearts and St Johnstone, I broke down with a back problem and the subsequent operation ruled me out for three months, including the League Cup final against Hibs. The result that day made up for the Euro agony we had suffered, especially the way we won the game.

Coisty was just two weeks into his comeback after breaking his leg when he proved that the doubters who said he was finished were well off the mark. The script was tailor-made for Ally, real comic book stuff. The match went to extra-time, with Durranty grabbing our goal, before an own goal from Dave McPherson levelled the score. The game was in stalemate and looked likely to be heading for penalty kicks when Coisty came off the bench. He had been taking a bit of stick from the lads because he had put on weight due to his long lay-off and had been nicknamed the Chunky Veteran in the dressing-room. But it was a classic moment when he launched that bulkier than normal frame into the air to send an overhead kick soaring past the helpless Jim Leighton and into the net, before landing on a well-cushioned behind and sprinting away for his customary celebrations.

I had met up with Stuart Munro before the match and we were in the back of the stand with my dad and brother and a pal of mine, Bill Andrews, and it was a great moment. The goal meant a lot to Ally and we partied in style in every pub in Paisley Road West afterwards. It turned out to be one of the few real highlights of the season.

The Ne'erday game against Celtic, which we won 4–2, was another one for the fans to savour. We demolished them, going up 3–0 in the first half hour, including two goals in the first four minutes. The heroes that day were Hateley, Mikhailitchenko who grabbed two, and our other Ukrainian star, Oleg Kuznetsov. Hateley was also on target in the League Cup semi-final when we scored another Old Firm victory at Ibrox, but on the whole, memorable performances and moments were certainly thinner on the ground than they had been in previous years.

After that traumatic experience against Dundee United, we still went on to win the title, but only by default: as it turned out that United game was our the last victory of the season. We didn't win a single match and as losing is always a bad habit to get into I thought it was a real worry for the final. We lost 2–1 to Motherwell the following week, drew 1–1 with Celtic with Alexei Mikhailitchenko grabbing our last goal of the season, and then lost 1–0 to Hibs and Kilmarnock and drew 0–0 with Dundee as we held our Six-in-a-Row party at Ibrox.

It turned out to be our worst goal drought in nearly a decade as we hadn't fired blanks in four successive games since then. We were crowned as champions again on 3 May at Easter Road, as Motherwell's defeat handed us the title, although technically we could still have been caught on goal difference. We didn't like to win it that way, but we had done the business over the campaign, even if we couldn't clinch it in style. It's far better to win it on your own terms, but all the boys were just delighted to get there at last and look forward to the final part of the Treble.

Our performances had been so unconvincing that when I joined the squad as they prepared at Turnberry the week before the Cup final, and Archie and Walter asked me to pick my team for the final, I really struggled. I had watched our League games with the exception of the clincher at Easter Road, as I was in London and had my op the next day. And I had to admit that I hadn't seen anyone, bar one or two, who had done enough to say that they would definitely be first down on the team sheet.

I had a really bad feeling about the final and it turned out to be right. In a totally lacklustre match, we finally handed it to United on a plate after a mix-up between Ally Maxwell and Dave McPherson which allowed Craig Brewster to score. Those two carried the can for our defeat, but the blame has to be shared. Normally, even if we lost a goal, we would have been able to score two in reply, but even Mark Hateley, who had found the net 30 times that season, couldn't turn things around.

We were all gutted to lose like that. Losing by the same scoreline to Celtic in 1989 had been bad, but this felt even worse. We went back to Ibrox for what would have been the party to end all parties and the boys tried to make the best of it, but the champagne had definitely gone a bit flat. I had a couple of pints, but ended up leaving early at around ten o'clock. I felt absolutely terrible and ended up being physically sick during the night, probably through the nervous tension of the day. It was even worse for me being in the stand that afternoon than if I'd been playing. I kept thinking that I should have postponed the op, played on and been able to do my bit and I got myself really wound up about it.

If we had less injuries we might have done it, and to get there after the problems we had would have been an even bigger achievement than our clean sweep of the previous year. But we simply weren't up to the task and the warning signs in the previous matches had turned out to be totally accurate, even though to be on the verge of it again and win two trophies out of three after all we'd gone through was still a fantastic achievement.

Graeme Souness always said that lucky teams can win the Cup while only good teams win the League. In United's case it certainly seemed to be true. Ivan Golac, through a much more relaxed approach, had captured a trophy that for all his success Jim McLean had never been able to bring to Tannadice. Golac liked to shoot his mouth off and afterwards he was saying this and that about Rangers, but they were nearly relegated that season and the following year, when Billy Kirkwood took over from Golac, it was too late to stop them slipping into the First Division. Recently Ivan's been in the press, declaring that if he was still in charge United would be challenging Rangers. Well, he failed to do that when he was there, so he should shut up and let Billy get on with it.

In hindsight I regret missing out on that final, but I believed the boys would still have enough in the tank to do it without me. Who knows how it could have turned out, even if I had made myself available for selection? But as always, I would rather have been on the park and given it 100 per cent. If you do that and still lose it takes some of the sting out of the defeat.

Chapter Fifteen

The Foreign Legion

Without doubt the player who made the most impact on last season was our great Dane, Brian Laudrup. He shone in a season which threatened to be over before it began with our devastating defeat against AEK Athens in the qualifying round for the Champions League.

But our other big-name summer signing that season, French star Basile Boli, turned out to be less of a hit – off or on the pitch. After that Greek tragedy we lost a couple of important games at home to Falkirk in the League Cup, blowing any Treble hopes we might have harboured right away, and then to Celtic. It was one bad week which felt more like a year and nearly ruined our season.

You can imagine how upset Walter was by all this and he's not shy at showing his feelings at the time. A dressing-room with a closed door can be just as scary a place to be with him as it ever was with Graeme Souness. But once he's said his piece, he accepts that you just have to get on with it and set your sights on other targets.

The failure to qualify for the Champions League was a blow to us all, but perhaps especially for our two signings that summer, Laudrup and Basile Boli, as there's no doubt that the fact that we were potential Champions League candidates swayed their decision to come to Ibrox.

Even in that week of three defeats the snipers were out for Brian, but after he got over that he was a revelation. One man can't carry a team, but his contribution was immense. He got into double figures in the scoring stakes and created roughly 75 per cent of our goals. It was an amazing series of displays, but it's a team game and you have to have people there to win the ball for him as well. But he was outstanding and won not only the Sportswriters Player of the Year award, but the PFA equivalent and an armful of accolades from supporters clubs up and down the country. Some people have said that he's only in the Premier Division because he couldn't make the grade in the tougher Italian Serie A. That's Scotland for you, we always like to knock successes. But Brian is enjoying a new lease of life here after Italy where he didn't really settle, on or off the pitch. He wasn't enjoying his football because the teams he was playing for wanted him to play in a very regimented way. He came to Rangers and the manager gave him a free role and let him play the way he wanted. Brian, or 'Lauders' to give him his Ibrox nickname, told me once that when he was with AC Milan the manager wouldn't let the full-back go over the halfway line, while he was supposed to cover the entire length of the wing without any support. Quite simply he didn't enjoy it and his family weren't happy there either.

There's a fair collection of winners' medals in our dressing-room, but Brian is the *only* one, apart from Alexei Mikhailitchenko, with a European Championship winners' medal, so for anyone to say he couldn't play like this in the Serie A is a joke.

Another important factor in his displays for Rangers is the fact that there is a closer-knit footballing community here. Around Ibrox, the players and their wives get on well, which has no doubt helped him settle in instead of being distanced from the local players the way it often happens in Italy. People in the West of Scotland are generally like that and I don't think I've heard any foreign or English players have a bad word to say about the place. But if he was inspirational on the pitch, there were other players ready to rise to the same heights.

Once we had put our early season hiccups behind us, the last three months of the year, when I was still recoving from injury, produced some breathtaking football. That was our best and most consistent period of the season. The manager had a settled side to choose from and the boys were all playing with confidence and we had a good understanding built up. I was thinking, 'How am I going to get back into a side like this when I'm fit?' They were doing exceptionally well. But fortunately for me, another injury let me back into the side in the new year.

I feel a lot more comfortable with the players we've signed this time round than last season. Another important figure for us was Alan McLaren, who had finally signed for us after a long period of speculation. His arrival and that of Gordan Petric the following close season may have hampered my chances of breaking off from my coaching duties to get a first team call, but I rate both of them very highly and the club needs players of this quality.

For someone of his age, Alan has already established himself as a Scotland regular and even in his Hearts days he was a mature player. When he first arrived, the manager had to move him around and used him at full-back, which isn't his best postition, but when he's in the centre of defence it's easy to see he's a player of real quality.

I have to be honest and admit that I wasn't such a big fan of Basile Boli. When you've seen a player in action and played against him, you think he'll do a job for you. But the only way to test it out is to sign him, and until you do that you never know just how he will fit in. I think everyone, from the chairman, manager, players and fans, was excited about Basile's arrival. And when you looked at his pedigree, over 50 caps for France and someone who had scored the winning goal in the European Cup final for a great Marseille team, it was fair to assume that he would be an asset. Unfortunately, it just didn't work out and some of his off-the-field antics turned into a bit of a French farce.

When we were knocked out so early in Europe, I don't think his heart was in it from then on. He just didn't fancy the job any more and I think you saw signs of that. Then there were a few comments attributed to him which didn't go down too well with the players. He claimed that they didn't take the games seriously enough and were laughing and joking around before big games, like the AEK match. And even though it was denied and he claimed to have been misquoted by the French magazine in question . . . when you break that bond with your team-mates, it's not the same any more. The majority of players who come, even foreigners, who don't know the traditions of Rangers, soon learn to respect them. I always felt that Basile didn't have that. He always felt he was bigger than the club and didn't have the love for the club that the rest of the guys have.

Look at Mark Hateley and what Rangers meant to him – and he's a player who's been with some of the biggest clubs in Europe in Milan and Monaco. Basile would never put the club before himself and to me that's a down side. Even during the season he was talking about winning League medals in every different country. I was surprised at him doing that while he was still under contract to Rangers. That's another sign of disrespect for the club.

And it could all have been so different.

During the first two pre-season games he played in, the buzz around the ground whenever he got the ball was incredible. But the fans soon found him out too and sadly, for someone who could have been a great Rangers player, he became someone who did all his talking off the park and hardly any on it, which was a major disappointment.

But the Gaffer will be the first to tell you that signing *any* player is a gamble: you just never know how they'll take to their new surroundings. And in Basile's case, that gamble didn't pay off. He would rather have been Basile Boli than a Rangers player. When the big man first signed for us it looked as if my appearances were going to be limited because of it. But even though you still want to be involved and prove a point about your own ability, my main reaction was 'Great, he can do a job for us'. It's the team and winning that matters, not the individual, but I don't think Big Baz shared the same view.

As I've said, probably the most offputting factor from his point of view was our European exit. But I wasn't too happy about that result myself and I was gutted to be ruled out, with Gary Stevens taking my place. But the manager had spotted that I wasn't 100 per cent fit physically or mentally, although I had convinced myself that I could do a job. Athens had quick players all the way through their side – from their full-backs to forwards, so that was the reason Gary was in. He had played well against Manchester United in the pre-season tournament, which probably swayed it.

But as is well documented, we just didn't have the blend right. Europe is our biggest target in every season now. We have to qualify or there's no buzz about the place – expectations are so high among fans and players. In Scotland we expect so much every year in European competition and we must be honest and admit we just haven't done ourselves justice at that level. But maybe that comes back to home, because there's no doubt you need tougher competition, on a more consistent basis, to battle-harden you for Europe and prepare you for that level. And it doesn't make it any easier when you're into European action before the domestic season has even begun.

At home it turned out to be just as tough. It's been said before that every game is a cup final for Rangers and it hit home that week, that apart from our own fans, everyone else in Scotland, and not just the football fans, but the media as a whole and commentators like Jock Brown, love to knock us down. We don't normally have results like that back to back so the press had a field day and of course, after all the hype and build-up, with the Champions League tantalisingly close again, our own fans were less than happy.

I can understand their disappointment in situations like that, but in the last few seasons Rangers have broken all sorts of records and I firmly believe they'll go on to break even more. So what I would say to all our supporters is that in times like that the players need your backing even more than ever. As the song says, 'No one likes us, we don't care . . .' There's no doubt we have to stick together.

How many times have you heard a Rangers manager asking publicly for other sides' help to defeat our nearest challengers and take points off them the way other managers do with us at the start of just about every season? Where other clubs are concerned, there's a big jealousy factor. Even when I was at Dundee and most of the guys there were Rangers fans, they always wanted to do so much better against Rangers than Celtic, because they were such a big club. I had read stories about Rangers being interested in me earlier in my career, but they never followed it up, so every time I faced them I had a point to prove, that I was as good as anything they had. If you read the match reports in the papers, there's not a week goes by that the keeper or some player hasn't had a blinder against us on the big stage that a capacity Ibrox provides and then has gone out the following week and had an absolute nightmare against Aberdeen, Motherwell or whoever.

Because of that factor, the pressure on our players is incredible, and that is something the home support fails to understand. Players don't set out deliberately to make a bad pass or miss a tackle, but because of the high standards that have been set, our fans seem to be far more critical. Our away support has always been tremendous, and although they turn up in huge numbers at Ibrox they need to play a more vocal part. Their backing gives the players a tremendous boost. I think we've lost a bit of atmosphere over the years at Ibrox, especially now it is all seated with the enclosure gone. And on days like those early season defeats, even when we deserve the abuse that's being hurled, it's important to remember that that kind of 'support' only helps the opposition.

Apart from that purple patch just before Christmas, the season didn't really hit too many highs, especially with our Treble chance and European hopes blown out so early. But in another hangover from the previous season, several of the boys went under the knife. Coisty had been out on and off for nearly two years, Mark Hateley had to have an op and I think he'd be the first admit that it knocked him out of his stride and it took him a while to battle back to his best.

Playing so many competitive games definitely takes its toll. Twenty-three of the boys finished the season with one type of injury or another, so to win the League was a major achievement, and believe me they don't get any easier. I underwent a hernia operation and struggled with a groin injury for most of the season.

My favourite moment from the season was half a game I played against Kilmarnock, as our usual drastic injury situation gave me a chance to get back in the side. I've never said to the manager that I hate any position, but I think he knows which ones they are, which blows out the 'I'll play anywhere' routine. But being honest, I've never really been too keen on that left midfield role. Having had two ops around the groin area, my movement was restricted and I'd been going up and down to the FA's rehabilition centre at Lilleshall. Our physio, Grant Downie, had given me a course of exercises to help and I'd spent hours just knocking a ball off a wall in the bowels of the stadium to improve my touch and movement, usually for at least an hour before training had even begun.

After a few months I felt a big difference. For a start, my touch was great! I felt comfortable going back into training. Even at my age after spending so many hours with the ball, my touch was bound to improve. With Robbo out, someone else moved into full-back and I took over wide on the left and enjoyed every second of it. The manager just told me to keep the ball in play and that Laudrup would be around. I did. We did the business and won 3–0. More importantly, from my point of view, it was the first time I'd ever played that position and felt good about it. And some time after that, when Miko was recovering from injury, there wasn't another naturally left-sided player around and I got the call again!

The sheer enjoyment of having that kind of role being able to get forward and see so much of the ball and being able to handle it was great after seasons spent grafting in the defence. There was no added pressure. You can only do your best and I think I surprised even myself. Having said that, I would have loved to have been at centre-half, but with Boli in there beside Goughie, there wasn't much chance, although it'd done me a turn being able to play in so many positions.

Richard had another great season and, once again, probably didn't get the credit he deserves. He is highly rated by all the players at Ibrox and the management, but for some reason some sections of the support don't give him his due. He's consistent, a great reader of the game and a great Rangers captain. But perhaps taking over the job from someone like Big Terry Butcher, who was more flamboyant and larger than life off the park, has hampered him. Basile was probably more of a marker at Marseille, with a sweeper behind him, so Goughie had to cover a lot of ground and the players will tell you just what a magnificent season he had.

The turning point in the League campaign came on Hogmanay when we beat Motherwell 3–1, thanks to goals from McCall, Durie and Laudrup. That virtually clinched it. The boys produced a good performance, as did 'Well, but we stuck to our task and Jukebox got a great third goal to finish it. That result saw off their challenge. They went into a slump after that before finishing second in the League and grabbing a place in Europe.

Motherwell have improved tremendously in recent seasons. From a side whose defensive attitude made them one of the most boring teams in the country, they have gradually acquired a better quality of player. Tommy McLean spent wisely and they're now a team which is challenging for honours every season instead of doing their damnedest to stay out of the relegation zone. I would say that last time round, under Alex McLeish, they provided our toughest challenges and played some nice football along the way.

From a personal point of view, the highlight was clinching the title against Hibs, because it meant I could keep a promise to my daughter Lauren. She's just five and Diana and I were shocked to find out that she would have to undergo an operation to correct a heart valve problem. We couldn't believe it at first, but a routine school medical revealed that she was suffering from co-ortation of the aorta which could lead to high blood pressure in later life. After nearly two months of worry she had a successful operation at Glasgow's Yorkhill Hospital for Sick Children, whose staff were brilliant.

I had promised to take her round the pitch with me if we won the title against Aberdeen the previous week. But her hospital date meant she would have missed out on that Dons game, so I was more than happy to wait until the Hibs match to start the celebrations. She loved it and it was a great day for me because of that.

It's not until something like that happens that you realise how unimportant football can be. She took everything else away. To win the League and get her out there for the celebrations was one of the most pleasurable experiences I've ever had in the game, especially as she made a full recovery after her operation.

I played on during that period, including a brief spell as captain against Celtic, before retiring injured. But I have to admit that I found it difficult for once to keep my mind 100 per cent on the game. I was up and down to the hospital all week. The manager had done me a turn by making me captain, but I was off early on after pulling a hamstring. A few minutes later I was desperate to be back on the pitch as we were ripped apart. Celtic were nothing special, but that was one of our worst performances of the season even though we had just won the League and it really hurt all the players and the fans.

Apart from that performance, where we didn't do ourselves credit, we won the League by a comfortable margin. And although the title was already in the bag, that defeat soured the celebrations. Another real downer, having gone out of the League Cup earlier in the season, was being dumped by Hearts in the Scottish Cup at Tynecastle in February. I felt really good going into that match and I was ready to play, but the manager stuck me on the bench. I was disappointed not to be involved from the first whistle. We got off to a bad start, with Colin Miller and Dave McPherson, who'd done a great job at Ibrox for us the season before, putting Hearts 2–0 up by half-time. But Brian Laudrup and Gordon Durie levelled the score and we got back on top before Kevin Thomas and John Robertson finished us off. Some of the papers noted afterwards that it was the first time I'd finished on a losing Rangers team for 22 months – since we lost to Aberdeen in May 1993, in fact. But really, as far as I'm concerned, that brief appearance didn't count as a defeat in personal terms. Getting off to such a poor start, and losing an early goal was a major kick in the teeth and from then on the die was cast. It's not Rangers style, and I hate to admit it now, but we should have played for a replay that night instead of charging up the park looking for a winner.

Every time we did, Hearts clobbered us again. We would pull one back, then they would hit back again. By the time I came off the bench it was too late to salvage anything. I always feel that if you're going to lose it's better to stand up and be counted and play the 90 minutes rather than coming on for the last ten and chasing the game. At 2–2 we should have hung on, but we let them back in and it was over and out – we'd missed the chance of making our fourth Scottish Cup final appearance in a row.

That day at Hampden is the biggest day of the season. Winning the League is great, but the Scottish Cup final is a tremendous experience. The week before it we always prepare at Turnberry. The build-up is great, right up to the morning of the match and then being on that pitch in a capacity stadium with the pipers marching up and down is wonderful. To miss out on a big glamour day like that is murder, and what made it worse was the fact that Hearts went on to lose out to First Division Airdrie in the semi-final. Without being arrogant, having beaten us and showing the spirit they did to go through, you would have expected them to go on and win it.

It may sound like sour grapes, particularly as Celtic were the eventual winners, but the final itself was a poor game. Airdrie didn't find the type of form that took them to their second final in four years and the Celts could only produce a solitary goal to capture the Cup. But if you win the match and collect your medal at the end of it, that's all that matters.

The biggest shock to everyone at Ibrox in that season, though, was the death of Davie Cooper. We heard on the radio in the dressing-room that Coop had been rushed to hospital after collapsing during filming of a coaching programme at Broadwood Stadium in Cumbernauld. At first we didn't realise the significance and thought, 'He'll pull through'. But it wasn't to be and Davie never regained conciousness. When we found out the full story, it became clear that he had little chance of recovery. It was a sad, sad blow for everyone.

My happiest memories of Coop are playing behind him at left-back when he was torturing defenders further up on the wing.

Everything Davie did looked so simple and he was a joy to play beside. You would make a run past him on the overlap and the ball was there for you. He had the knack of always finding you with a deft pass. He was simply one of the best players I've ever seen or had the pleasure to play with. Even now, months afterwards, it's still hard to believe that someone so young has gone.

Davie always said he didn't fancy moving into coaching once his playing days were over. But once he had got a taste of it, he changed his mind and he was thoroughly enjoying the experience. He left Rangers in 1989, finishing his Ibrox career on a high and even though that was nearly six years before his untimely death, you still felt as if he had never really been away from the place. He would probably have been shocked at the emotion his death caused up and down the country. The scarves and floral tributes at the Ibrox gates and then the incredible turn-out at his funeral in Hamilton when the streets were lined, were incredible. I left it for a few days before I went to see the tributes which came from our fans, Celtic fans and clubs all over Britain. It was very touching.

Davie was a big star, but at heart he was always just one of the punters. That was the way he wanted to live. He never bothered about money. There were always players at the club concerned about bonuses and every penny going, but Coop hated all of that. All he wanted to do was pick up a wage, enjoy his football, have a bet and have a pint.

People have called him a legend before and since . . . a boy like that. His death affected everyone who knew him and everyone connected with Rangers and Motherwell, and also people who had never met him – but still knew him. It says so much that he touched so many people, even those who had only seen him on television. It was heartbreaking then and it's still hard to believe now. But he's left a lot of memories filled with a whole lot of magic moments.

One of my favourites was the devastating free-kick he scored in the 1987 Skol Cup final at Hampden. Even in slow motion replay it still screams past the Aberdeen wall. There was also the terrific flick which set up an Ian Durrant goal against Celtic, but you could go on forever. If you ask other people they would all have special memories of their own, not just of goals, but of an incisive pass or a graceful turn or bit of ball control.

Around Ibrox he was nicknamed Albert Tatlock, amongst other things, after the grumpy character in *Coronation Street*, because of all the moaning he used to do. He was always ready with a caustic remark, but you couldn't meet a nicer guy.

We all shed a tear or two, but it must be even worse for his family to have him taken away so early. For anyone to have known him or played with him was a pleasure. Scotland has lost a national treasure, but he'll always be in our hearts.

Chapter Sixteen

Standing Count

I've had my fair share of ups, downs and injury scares over the years. But what no one outside my family and the club knows is that in the summer of 1994 I was told to hang up my boots – or risk having a knee replacement operation.

Following on from the hernia problems I had at the end of the previous season I had the knee cleaned out by Dr John Browatt, a top Harley Street surgeon, which I thought was fairly routine. But I was stunned when he turned to me and said: 'I think you should consider an alternative form of employment.' He warned me that the wear and tear of my right knee over the years, and the arthritis which has built up in it, means that it will result, hopefully a number of years down the line, in a knee replacement.

I was shocked and asked: 'If I look after myself, how long?'

'I would advise that as soon as you can, call it a day, but at the most a couple of years,' came the reply, which left me even more stunned.

After being told that I returned to Ibrox and broke the news to the manager who simply asked me what I wanted to do. 'I just want to play,' was all I could tell him.

'Then I'll stick with you,' he said simply.

Walter's been great. There hasn't been one bit of pressure on me, he's let me get on with things and played me when required and when I was fully fit. And he also took a great weight of my mind by offering me a coaching position at the club, so I wasn't forced to carry on playing week in, week out, to try and keep my place in the team. That could have made matters worse.

Ironically, before that visit, I wasn't too worried. The knee wasn't the issue. Since our treble-winning season, I've had *five* operations in two years. The biggest worry was my back when I ruptured a disc, because the surgeons had to work around my spine. But I came back from that only to have a string of problems with my groin and a hernia, all of which were down the left side and in retrospect probably related.

Since I had my last knee operations in my early twenties they haven't caused me any real problems. They're not very pretty to look at, but then neither is my face. Because of that, the news was a real shock. But I was 32 when I found out and if I carry on for another couple of years I'll be the same age as most players when they retire anyway. When you compare that to the tragedy which hit Scott Nisbet and robbed him of what should have been the finest years of his career, it's nothing. Nissy's pelvic problem, and the speed at which it ended his Ibrox days, left everyone at Ibrox gutted for the big man, who was a great servant to the club and a better player than a lot of the fans, among whom he had a cult status, gave him credit for.

John McGregor is another player, whose career was cut short by a knee injury, and there have been plenty of players with other clubs who've suffered the heartache of having their career ended just when they've had their first taste of glory. So I'm just thankful that I've had so many good years under my belt first. Even if I had done what Scott was forced to, and stop immediately the problem was diagnosed, I could still be facing problems in ten years time, so I've decided to carry on for the meantime. I still train every day with the youngsters and I'm feeling fitter now than I have done in the past three years. I've restricted myself a bit, but I'm active every day and, more importantly, all day. Instead of going home after training and lying on the couch, I'm constantly on the move and keeping myself ticking over, which will hopefully prolong my career. If I just stopped and there was muscle wastage through a lack of exercise, there would be less protection around my knee and the effects of that could be just as damaging.

I know myself that after having both cartilages removed as a teenager and getting by with it, then there had to be problems.

In those days they removed the whole cartilage. Nowadays if it's just a small tear they'll tidy it up. With me the joints are just rubbing together, there's no shock absorber there. But anyone who knows me will tell you that quitting, even when I'm ahead, isn't one of my strong points. And I know that If I look after myself, and avoid giving it a pounding every day in training, I can keep going. We've got a new gym at the club and that equipment means I can compensate by working in there. This is your job. Your life. And it's hard to turn your back on it just like that. If my knees are going to pack up, they'll pack up, but at the moment I'm on a high every day and I'll carry on for as long as possible.

Ray Wilkins always used to say, 'Your body is your bank.' You can't go overdrawn and you have to keep making regular deposits, and that's what I've been trying to do.

The news that May gave me a real jolt and even though I've always worked hard in training, I'm looking after myself even more carefully now in terms of watching what I eat and getting the proper amount of rest. I've been used to people doubting my fitness throughout my career, so my response was to shrug my shoulders and get on with it.

Since I was given the bad news, I've played for the reserves and turned out several times last season for the first team. I regard every single one of those games as a bonus. And I'm still ready to answer the call for the first team when it comes.

Chapter Seventeen

Simply The Best

I've played alongside a lot of top-quality players at Ibrox and picking my own dream team, made up of guys I've played alongside personally, is no mean feat. The club has been lucky enough to have attracted some of the best players in Britain in recent seasons, and more recently, some of the best in Europe as well. Here's the line-up I would choose: Goram, Stevens, Robertson, Gough, Wilkins, Butcher, Laudrup, Ferguson, McCoist, Hateley, Cooper. Subs: Woods, Walters, Durrant.

And here's why.

In goals it's not too difficult a decision. My number one would be ANDY GORAM who has been simply the best of the lot in my time at the club. He's showed his class time and time again, week in and week out.

The most recent memory for fans will be that Coca-Cola Cup tie against Celtic at Parkhead when he pulled off a string of magnificent saves to put us into the semi-finals, but since he signed from Hibs, he's been producing that level of performance every other week. Chris Woods was a hard act to follow – I thought he was an exceptional keeper – but Andy's form in the last few years has been nothing short of brilliant. He has great presence and stands up to strikers really well, forcing them to decide what their next move will be and making it as difficult as possible by not committing himself too early.

Off the park he can be a moodier Blue than even Davie Cooper was – some days you don't even want to go near him – but in general he's different class. People read a lot of things about Andy in the press, but he's a great lad and once he goes on that park he's totally tuned in and focused. I love slating goalies, but it's hard to do that when you're playing in front of one of the best in the business.

When we won the League title in 1994, the night we lost to Hibs at Easter Road, I was down in London to have a groin operation the next day. Andy, myself and football agent Murdo Mackay were out at a nice restaurant and afterwards had the champagne on ice as we continually dialled home for results. When we found out Motherwell had lost and the title was ours it was party time again. I had been told not to drink after midnight, so I crammed in plenty before then. The party got noisier, and the highlight of the evening came when Andy leaned over to me and told me in a broad Lancashire stage whisper: 'Bomber, we better keep it down a bit, we don't want those English guys over there at the bar to find out we're Scots.'

Recently Andy took a bit of stick over his decision to withdraw from the Scotland squad because he didn't feel 100 per cent mentally for the game in question. But what people forget is that, like Ally, Andy was injured while doing his bit for the national team against Greece and missed a lot of big games for Rangers. He's never let Scotland down and is totally committed to their cause, even with an accent like that!

Wearing the number two shirt would be GARY STEVENS. In all my time at Ibrox he's been without doubt the best right back we've had. He had terrific stamina to sprint up that right wing into a forward position and then be back in time to make covering tackles using his terrific pace. He might not have been the best user of the ball, but he gave the team terrific options. Graeme Souness said when he did the deal with Everton to bring Gary to Ibrox that he'd signed the best right back in Britain and when Gary was at his peak I don't think he was wrong. He did a great job for England too and had a lot of experience at international level as he used his sheer athleticism to control the right flank. Gary was probably the fittest guy I've seen in my time at Ibrox although Richard Gough wouldn't be far behind in those terms. Like a lot of us, Stevo liked a night out, but he would play hard and work hard and after a night out he would be the first guy in at training the next morning and pushing himself harder than ever. When the club signed players of his calibre, experienced internationalists and big names down south, I thought that maybe they would come and rest on their laurels, but it didn't take me long to change my mind. Even in training, guys like Gary were really competitive.

TERRY BUTCHER and RICHARD GOUGH would be my automatic choices in the centre-back roles. Richard's reading of the game is second to none and the amount of covering work he does is a tremendous asset to any team. Everyone he plays alongside – as well as both Walter Smith and Graeme Souness – appreciates just how good a player he is, although he sometimes doesn't get the credit he deserves. He has been a major player in the club's success and has won a tremendous amount of trophies as captain. The three-at-the-back system we're using at the moment seems to suit him and at the start of the 1995/96 season he was looking better than ever.

Goughie's a great leader but I'd probably make Terry captain. Big Butch was an inspirational character on and off the field and a real hero to Rangers fans. Everyone looked up to him and he had an incredible stature within the game. He did a superb job for the club and I doubt if the Souness revolution would have been just as successful without the big man at the heart of the defence. He had great defensive qualities and was good in the air, but could also rip open opposing defences with those 60-yard balls he used to love to ping forward, finding a man without even looking. His 77 caps for England as well as the honours he won at Ibrox tell the story, and leading the club to the championship at Pittodrie in his first season as skipper and that daft hat he wore when we won the League at Tannadice were moments he will always be remembered for. It was a great honour for me to play alongside a guy like that.

At left-back DAVID ROBERTSON just pips Stuart Munro for a place in the starting line-up. Stuart did a great job and saw off a number of contenders for that position. He was very underrated, but I have to go for Robbo. He's got devastating pace and can be a real threat up front with that powerful shot of his. With he and Gary grafting on the wings, Goughie and Butcher would control the middle. Like Gary Stevens, Robbo hardly ever misses a game and has clocked up a tremendous number of appearances since he signed from Aberdeen.

Robbo must be one of the richest men in Scotland by now because he certainly doesn't spend his own money. He's got a really dry sense of humour and has fitted in well at Ibrox, but on a night out he can change from being one of the quietest men in the dressing-room to the Tasmanian Devil.

In midfield my task is even tougher. Guys like Trevor Steven, Derek Ferguson, Ian Durrant, Graeme Souness, Nigel Spackman, Piet Huistra, Alexei Mikhailitchenko, Stuart McCall and now Paul Gascoigne, have all played a vital part in our success over the years. But I can only pick four, so I'm going to stick my neck out and name BRIAN LAUDRUP, IAN FERGUSON, RAY WILKINS and DAVIE COOPER, who've all starred in successful sides of the Eighties and Nineties.

I've got a lot of happy memories of Mark Walters, who was a classy winger with some great ball skills and the ability to score important goals and deliver pinpoint crosses. His cross for Mark Hateley to score in the 1991 title decider against Aberdeen is a timeless moment He also notched one in the 5–1 game against Celtic and scored another in an Old Firm match direct from a corner. But it's difficult to see past Brian Laudrup, who's one of the most gifted players we've ever had and can win matches on his own. Despite the crowd-pleasing skills he possesses, Brian doesn't do anything extra in terms of training. The boys call him Long Body, because he's got this massive torso. But his legs still manage to produce an electric burst of pace over 20 yards.

A lot of people in Denmark thought he was mad to come and play in Scotland, but he had an extemely successful first season at Ibrox and looks as though he's really enjoying his time here. He can express himself and has more freedom than he ever had with Bayern Munich, Fiorentina or AC Milan.

Away from football, Brian's a very down to earth and intelligent guy who mixes well with the team. On nights out he used to be away early with Mark Hateley as they had further to travel to Helensburgh from the city, but he paid for lack of practice when we went to Monaco at the end of the season. On the park he's always running rings round people, but when you're on your hands and knees in a hotel corridor it's kind of difficult to do that.

Inside of Brian I'd go with my very underrated former room-mate IAN FERGUSON. Fergie's had plenty of injury worries which have stopped him having a really long run in the team over the years, but the strength and work-rate he brings to midfield is vital. He can go forward and get you goals, but he's also a great ball-winner and does a lot of tackling back to help out the defence too. It was a toss-up between him and Stuart McCall, who has also given great service to the club since he signed from Everton, and of course Durranty, whom I've got to leave out of the starting line-up for tactical reasons.

I've roomed with Fergie for a number of years now, probably because no one else will put up with his moaning. He complains that I'm a control freak and always have to have my finger on the button when we're watching TV. But he's a soap opera freak and that's why I keep a tight grip on the channel changer at all times. Like me, Fergie's also one of the most superstitious guys at Ibrox. Andy Goram puts some faith in lucky charms and I've been well served by the tape I wind round my socks. That started when I first came back from my Achilles injury in 1991. I had to cut off the ankle support on my shinpads and needed to hold the pads in position, so out came the tape and it's stayed ever since. Fergie's even worse. If he sees a magpie first thing in the morning he'll spend all day desperate to spot another because of the old 'one for sorrow' routine.

Beside him would be RAY WILKINS who was also, unbelievably underrated by some throughout his career. Ray oozes class and really ran the show in his time at Ibrox. He was a player who would take the ball and then let it do all the work. Ray dictated everything we did during a game and would supply the ammunition for the wide men. When I first saw him I thought his game was just square balls all the time, but once I had played alongside him I realised just how good he was. His work-rate was immense. He would lose his marker, get on the ball and make a slide rule pass. The greatest compliment I can pay him is to say that we've never had anyone since who could do the same job as he did. Defenders never had to make more than a ten or 15-yard pass as Razor was always there to pick it up. I don't mean any disrespect to other lads who go about their business differently, but when he was there you never had to play a long ball. He's another whom the fans haven't forgotten since he moved on.

It was a great pleasure to play beside Ray, apart from one occasion during an Old Firm match when he and Coisty nearly came to blows. I had been drafted into the midfield for that match and during it I kept pushing forward to take on a man, leaving Ray to fill in the gap I had left. He was going absolutely crazy and kept screaming at me. I wasn't too bothered as we were ahead, and you can't ask for more in any Old Firm game, but Coisty was less than impressed. 'Bomber! Bomber . . . Hook him. Don't let him talk to you like that,' was the cry from the far end of the pitch. As we headed down the Parkhead tunnel at half-time I told him to leave it, but he was absolutely raging with Ray and was ready to have a go in the dressing-room. He gave the wee man absolute pelters, before finally being calmed down. Looking back, the whole thing was hilarious, especially when you consider that Ray is a real gentleman off the park. That was the one time he went overboard.

On the left wing there's only one man you can pick and that's DAVIE COOPER. He had great vision and with the pace of Davie Robertson to back him up the two of them together would have been sensational. Coop would go off on a mazy run and when his legs started to go he would lay on a perfect pass for you.

Davie had the lot and as well as the spectacular goals he was capable of delivering he had the ball control and technical skills that just aren't seen in many Scottish players these days. At dead ball situations, corners or free-kicks, whatever he was aiming for he would hit. He was one of the few you could say were worthy of that overused 'world class' tag. Davie was a genius. I'm grateful to have so many fond memories of him. On his day, even Laudrup couldn't match him.

Up front we've got another player who thinks he's a genius when it comes to scoring goals and when you look at his record, it's hard to argue. Step forward ALLY McCOIST MBE, Golden Boot(s) and just about every scoring record in Scottish Football. I think Ally's only got one or two goalscoring records he hasn't beaten in his time at Ibrox and as he'll tell you himself, he's the ultimate predator. I can never forget his contribution during our Treble-winning season where he scored a total of 49 goals before breaking his leg and missing the title run-in and Scottish Cup final. Whenever we win the title or the Cup, you can see guys who have played the whole season and then missed out at the last. Even though you played 30 or 40 games in a given season, to miss out on the celebrations means you don't really feel a part of it, even though you've as much right to celebrate as anyone. Some of the guys in our championship-winning teams over the last seven years have made only their second or third appearance that term, but have been there for all the adulation and been captured by photographers in the team group. Others have done it all through the season, but now they're on the sidelines and missed that special day. I've been there myself and it hurts, so I could really sympathise with Coisty when it came round to the Treble-winning party.

I've had plenty of good times off the park with Ally, in fact I could probably fill another book just on some of the fun we've had on team nights out over the years. One of the best days ever came during an end of season trip to Marbella when we started off on a champagne breakfast at a quiet bar. Seven hours later, the place was packed, with Ally doing his renowned Bruce Springsteen repertoire and singing almost non-stop, with everyone in the place joining in. It was a magic day and the previous evening was also notable for McCoist laying bets with everyone that he would go for a swim in the harbour among the yachts. Having been helped back out by two Spanish police, covered in grease and God knows what else, he was horrified the next morning to spot baby sharks swimming around in the absolutely filthy water. He was even more upset when he found out that none of the boys were prepared to pay up.

I've actually got a theory that the MBE at the end of his name stands for More Boiled Eggs. Another night out in the Steps Bar featured a drinking game involving passing a short round your head glued to your hand with the vacuum caused by setting it alight. After too many rounds of this, including one where Nigel Spackman managed to empty the contents over his head, I spotted a jar behind the bar containing one lonely and nearly rotten pickled egg which was well past it's sell-by date. Matt, the barman, popped it in a glass, covered it with Drambuie, and McCoist demanded that as it was his stag night he should be the one to attempt this next feat. He thought it was just an ordinary boiled egg, but took just one bite before spraying the assembled company's best clobber with the contents.

Even though he's played with a list of striking partners as long as your arm, I'd have to pair Ally with MARK HATELEY, who, pound for pound, was one of Souness's best signings. They scored more goals together over the years than any other partnership and they complemented each other perfectly. With Hateley getting on the end of crosses from the wide men, Ally was the ideal man to hoover up any chances around the box, usually the six-yard box, time after time. Hateley took a lot of stick in his first season at the club, most of which was unjustified as he was battling back from an ankle injury he picked up at Monaco. He took flak for almost the entire season until he finally won the fans over with his two goals against Aberdeen on the final day. That season changed so many things for the club and Mark. His first goal, that unforgettable header, made him a real hero and since then he's scored a lot of priceless goals, and later, when Ally was out injured, his goals carried the team for a long period. I had a great relationship with Mark in his time at Ibrox, even though we're from totally different backgrounds. Mark might have made the odd million or two in his career, but when he gets on to the park the only thing that matters to him is the game. He loves playing and he loves scoring.

At 34, the injuries and knocks which he used to shrug off caught up on him a bit more just before he left to join QPR and I would say his best spell was probably 18 months before that when he was in magnificent form for us. He was a proud guy and you could see some signs of frustration at not being able to win balls he would have done in the past. No one can go on forever, but his move to London will be a good one for him. It's another challenge and a chance to prove to people down there that he can score goals in the Premiership. I wish him well, and I'm sorry to see him go as I'm now the guy at the club with the least hair.

Before Mark left, there was a long-term rumour about him having a dressing-room bust-up with Duncan Ferguson after Duncy cut off the sleeves of his famous Versace suits. It's a nice story, but that's all it is. It simply never happened. But they did have a very minor clash at training in Il Ciocco not long after Duncan broke the transfer record to sign for Rangers. Fergie was the young pretender and Mark put him in his place, throwing him about like a rag doll on the training pitch.

On the bench, which would be larger than UEFA rules if I had my way, the first two names would be Walters and Durrant. Durranty's probably still in the huff at not getting into the starting line-up, but I rate the wee man very highly and both of them are capable of bringing a bit of magic to midfield any time you want. Without Durrant and McCoist I doubt if Rangers would have been as successful over the years.

As reserve goalkeeper I'd choose Woodsy who, as I've said, was a terrific keeper and one who set a new British shut-out record of 12 games during his Rangers days.

Also on the bench, I'd have to cheat a bit and bring in John Greig as player/coach. I didn't have the pleasure of playing alongside John, but he was a big hero of mine when I was younger and even though his playing days might be behind him, he'd be a great asset to the dressing-room with his wealth of experience. The only problem is keeping him and Durrant apart as Ian loves to wind him up and vice versa. 'Tell us again about Celtic's nine-in-a-row, John,' and so on. But having been at Ibrox during those years, Greigy's never slow to remind players that it's changed days and just how much flying that championship-winning flag at Ibrox should mean, even though it's now come to be almost expected of us every year.

Also on the bench would be kitmen Jimmy Bell and George 'Doddie' Soutar. Jim would be in charge of the mobile phone communications link (as I'm bound to have been banished to the stand) and Doddie for his cups of tea, moans, and his photographic memory of the good old days at Ibrox, from the 1928 Scottish Cup win onwards!

I'm taking on the manager's role myself as I couldn't separate Graeme and Walter. Both have worked miracles for Rangers and brought success to the club in their own way, but just like comparing the stars of the Sixties to players now, it's impossible as you're talking about two different eras of success at Ibrox. But I think they would both agree with the majority of my selections. Unlike me, they've both forked out hard cash for the same players over the years!

Chapter Eighteen

The Coach

My new role at Ibrox as youth and reserve team coach was only announced last May, but I had known about the chance of a backroom role when I signed my previous contract, just after our first sortie into the Champions League in 1993. The Gaffer told me then that he was considering bringing me on to the coaching staff and that was a great boost as I headed towards the final whistle on my playing career.

I signed a new one-year playing contract last summer and I was delighted to do so. I could have perhaps taken the same route as Davie Cooper and moved to another team in search of First Division football. But as far as I was concerned that idea was a non-starter and after chats with the boss and John Greig, I didn't fancy moving, especially to a First Division side. I would much rather finish my playing career at the top with Rangers, and having the chance to move into coaching at Ibrox as well as being on stand-by for a first team slot has been a terrific combination.

I still have first team ambitions and I've worked hard to keep myself fit and ready to answer the call if and when it comes. But the days of a regular spot in the first team are over and I accept that. I'm happy to play a similar role to Davie Dodds, who still turned out a few times for the first team when he was moved into coaching.

Walter has been 100 per cent behind me and I'm grateful to him for giving me the opportunity. The first developments came at the end of last season when Billy Kirkwood's move to Tannadice to take over the Dundee United hot seat looked to be on the cards. The Gaffer told me I was first in line for his job if he did decide to move to Dundee and if it didn't happen, there would still be another year's playing contract on the table. He also offered me the chance to go elsewhere and make a few quid by signing for another club, but I wasn't slow to tell him that I'd much rather stay at Ibrox.

I think both of us were happy with the new arrangement and it's nice to be offered the chance to get the best of both worlds while I'm still playing. It also means I get my initials on my training kit these days instead of a number and I've moved from the first team dressing-room into the coaches' room further along the corridor at the start of the tunnel. Walter was in a similar situation during his Tannadice days when Jim McLean allowed him to start coaching during the tail end of his playing career and I owe him a lot for giving me a similar chance.

Billy Kirkwood wished me all the best when he moved and it's been great to work alongside John McGregor, who's been involved with the reserves since a bad knee injury cut short his career, and of course, Davie Dodds. Both of them have gone out of their way to show me the ropes. John Greig has also been a great help and is always there with some advice if you need it. For me it's the ideal way to bring down the curtain on nearly eight years at Ibrox.

I'm still as enthusiastic coming through the front door on a Monday as I ever was and hopefully that's something I can instil in our younger players. For the young players coming to the club straight from school it's a real shock to the system as they're used to whatever training they did with their boys clubs, not to training every day. The main factor is they have to enjoy it and even though they're working alongside some big names, you can't allow them to get too big for their boots.

A lot of lads think because they've been signed by Rangers they've got it made, when really the hard work is just beginning. Even at other clubs, like Dundee and Hamilton, I've seen youngsters have their heads turned by the fact that they're playing football for a living. But there, and at Ibrox, it's tough to stay on board and go on to make it through the ranks to the first team.

The toughest part of the coaching job is likely to be at the end of the season when John and I have to make room for a new intake of kids and let some of the older reserve players move on. Having said that, even if they don't go on to win first team honours with Rangers, the whole set-up makes sure they get a great apprenticeship in the game which can only stand them in good stead at other clubs.

Since I started, I have loved every minute and I'm spending even more time at Ibrox than before, though I have to admit it is a wrench not to be part of the dressing-room scene, and the crack among the first team squad, any more. My wife will tell you that I'd be there seven days a week if I was allowed, and throughout my Rangers career I've always been one of the first into the dressing-room every morning about quarter past nine, before training started at 10. Now, I'll drop Lauren off at school at eight-thirty and be walking up the marble staircase for quarter to nine. I'll be in for a warm-up or some physio before Coisty has even opened his eyes.

Ibrox has undergone a terrific transformation since I used to go there as a boy and even since the mid-Eighties. It's a massive club, but there's still a family atmosphere and the players mix well with the office staff, Laura, the manager's secretary, and the girls in the kitchen, most of whom, like Tiny who's in charge of feeding the hungry hordes, have been there for years.

There's usually time for a quick morning cuppa, courtesy of Doddie, whom we like to wind up by telling him it's too strong. Then it's time to head out for training, though usually Coisty manages to hold up the proceedings by arriving at ten seconds to ten, having undressed in the car on the way and leaving himself time for at least a 30-second warm-up.

The great thing about the Ibrox dressing-room is the patter. The banter is something that everyone misses when they leave and every player who retires will tell you that not being there leaves a big gap in their life. If you don't enjoy training and your job, particularly at that level, then you don't deserve to be there and the laughter level is usually nothing short of hysterical. McCoist and

Durrant aren't exactly shy types and with Paul Gascoigne in there now it's even better.

I still feel privileged to have been a part of that and I'm always aware of the history of the place. The dressing-room still has the original wood panelling and hooks, especially designed for bowler hats, so the ghosts of other generations of Light Blue heroes are never far away. It helps keep your feet on the ground to realise just some of the great players who've been there and maybe shared the same peg as yourself down the years and if you want to stay at the top in this game you can't forget where you've come from.

I've been fortunate that right throughout my playing career my family have been 100 per cent behind me and a lot of my memories wouldn't mean as much if I hadn't had them to share them with. My dad and brother watch as many games as they can, but my mum, after a couple of experiences in with the bears at Old Firm games, prefers to watch matches on TV. She found the swearing and atmosphere a bit too much to handle. She also hates it if she hears anyone giving me abuse, whereas my dad and brother will usually enter into a discussion on the subject.

My grandfather gave up his love of junior football when I started playing and he came to see me play at Ibrox a couple of times. I don't think he could even see as far as the park, but he just loved being there. After he died, my gran would get out the scrapbook he kept of my performances. He used to cut out everything from the papers, stick it in and take it into his room to read over and over again. That brings it home to you, that for all the happy memories your family have given you, you can give them a wee bit back.

I'm sure the rest of the lads in the team who've been brought up with the club, like Ian Ferguson, Ian Durrant, Ally McCoist, Goughie and now Charlie Miller, know exactly what I'm talking about and know what it is to play for Rangers and how much it means to a lot of people close to them that they're involved and doing well along with the team. It was great for my dad when I joined Rangers to get the chance to meet the Ibrox legends like Jock 'Tiger' Shaw, Bob McPhail, Willie Thornton and Willie Waddell.

Mr Thornton and Mr Waddell, as you always addressed them, are sadly gone now, but right up until their deaths they still loved being a part of things at Ibrox. Both are a great loss – they *were* Rangers. Bob McPhail still comes to reserve matches and when you listen to him telling stories about the old days in the players' lounge over a cup of tea you can see it in his eyes that the kid inside is right back there at the 1928 Cup final or whatever, enjoying every second of those memories. John Greig is another guy who's still part of the club nearly 40 years after he first arrived and he'll tell you that those kind of recollections are a great thing to have.

Even the dress codes instilled by managers like the great Bill Struth are still in force. I met Gazza in Las Vegas just before he signed and he said, 'What's all this about having to wear a collar and tie every day?' I explained that it was part of the club's tradition and everybody stuck to it. 'I'm getting the biggest kipper tie ever, then,' he said. 'I'm going to break myself in gently.'

But even someone who's as big a star as he is quickly realises that Rangers are a very special club and you could see it when he first signed that he was desperate to be involved. Since Gazza has arrived, we've got another joker in the pack, and you could do a half-hour sitcom every morning with the material you get in there. Having said that, football grounds are like any big factory or office up and down the country. The same type of Glasgwegian or Scottish humour that's made Billy Connolly famous, with his tales from his shipyard days, is there at all clubs at all levels, although there are a lot of unconcious comedians around as well.

Coming back on the bus one day from Aberdeen, Ian Durrant was missing out on some of the chat from the back of the bus. 'What's that you're saying, Duncy? I can't hear a thing, I'm as deaf as a bat,' he said.

If the lads enjoyed that one, a few miles down the road it got even better. Duncan Ferguson was taking a bit of stick over his ability to handle a beer, but as he told the company: 'I'll tell you what lads, I can drink like a chimney.'

Even better was to follow on another bus journey, this time to training. As we headed towards the Clyde tunnel and the training ground Mark Hateley told us he had to watch his speed on the way in in the mornings because: 'The place is crawling with those plain-clothed police cars.' 'What are they wearing?' asked McCoist. 'Corduroys?'

And during a reserve game at Ibrox one day Billy Kirwood was heard to scream at one of the young lads: 'Get on your bike and start running.'

As you know, pre-season with Dundee could be a riot and it's the same at Ibrox. During one memorable trip to the Il Ciocco training camp in Italy, Scott Nisbet had us in stitches when he went off in search of some suntan lotion and the first guy he asked was Mark Walters. The same week, Nissy and Sandy Robertson could be spotted taking full advantage of the centre's excellent fitness and health facilities . . . by using the sunbeds while it was 80 degrees outside.

And it's not just Ibrox that can provide a fund of stories that will probably keep Coisty in after-dinner speaking material until the end of his days. Over the years I've been a regular at the SFA-run coaching courses at Largs, having passed my A and B coaching badges. There, the professional players mingle with amateurs, juniors and people in charge of school teams and they're all very keen. But when you actually have to take charge of a side and give them a pre-match pep talk and tell them how you want to play it, things sometimes don't go according to plan. Quotes like: 'The back four are all at sixes and sevens' and from a senior pro who I have to name – step forward John Gahagan – 'The best form of attack is defence.' You'd never guess he used to play for Motherwell.

During a match, one budding coach was heard to instruct his side to 'look over your shoulder to see the guy in front of you'. Gordon, a guy who runs an amateur side, also provided the classic 'The counter attack starts as soon as we lose the ball'.

Along with the laughs, the knowledge I've picked up on those courses has been invaluable in helping me develop my coaching skills and to give Andy Roxburgh his due, when he was involved he organised things well and had it down to a tee.

The news of my appointment to the coaching staff was intially delayed because of our worries over Lauren and her heart operation. Both Diana and I were absolutly stunned when we found out that a routine check by her school doctor had discovered a heart valve problem which could be serious in later life if it wasn't operated on. From that moment onwards we couldn't think about anything else and neither could our families. When I carried her down to the theatre she was petrified and I wasn't far away from tears myself. It is hard to explain just how bad it was to see her afterwards in intensive care with all sorts of tubes and wires around her.

The problem was co-ortation of the aorta, where a blockage to the main valve in the heart led to a weak blood supply. We spent a lot of anxious hours camping out at the hospital and I wasn't far away from ending up in a padded cell, I was so worried.

In Lauren's room was a picture of a teddy bear's picnic and it was a magic moment when she asked me to take it down because it was making her hungry and she was starving. I knew then she was over the worst. I couldn't believe that she came out of it smiling, as it was a lot for a five-year-old to go through. When she came out of the hospital I overheard her on the phone to her wee pal, Christopher. She had had a loose tooth taken out while she was in hospital in case it created any complications and she told him: 'You'll never believe what's happened to me. I was in the hospital and the tooth fairy came . . .'

I didn't know whether to laugh or cry.

If you had to ask me what was my biggest ever high, it would have to be that moment when I knew she was on the road to recovery and having her out on the pitch when we celebrated six in a row. And although I owe a lot to a lot of people within the game, the people I have to say the biggest thanks to are Dr Alan Houston, the surgeon, Dr Morgan Jamieson, and all the staff at Yorkhill Hospital, as well as our Dr Fiona Marshall and Dr Rodger from the school and, of course, our families who kept us both going.

I'd also like to thank all the supporters who took time to pass on their best wishes and who've always been simply the best as far as I'm concerned, and even some of my biggest rivals in the game who took the trouble to ask how Lauren was doing. The manager was great, allowing me to play and take my mind off it and he also made me captain for the Old Firm game around that time, even though I had to come off injured.

All this was going on around the same time Coop died and one afternoon Coisty and I must have driven away all the customers in a city centre pub when we stayed on together as the rest of the team carried on with a day out. Ally was still emotional about Coop, I wasn't much better, and the barman must have thought we were a right pair, sitting crying into our beer together. It was a period of my life that put a lot of things into perspective and even though this book's about football I could write a book on that one subject on its own.

After what we went through, if I had to choose between having Lauren go through something like that and all the medals and money in the world, I would still be a welder. This book would be a hell of a lot shorter, but I'd still like to dedicate it to the bravest wee girl in the world. I would have sacrificed the lot to have her well. But then, I know how lucky I am to have both.

I've got fond memories of just about every moment of my time at Douglas Park, Dens Park and Ibrox Park. I haven't hung up my boots as far as the first team is concerned and I wouldn't rule me out of a return just yet. But I'm loving my new role as a coach and now I'm starting to take pleasure from the game in a different way, in the achievements of our young players, who are the stars of tomorrow, particularly if they do something on the park that you've tried to instil in them and it works.

However, it's still nice to hear the roar of the crowd. And it was even nicer to get off to a flyer in my first Old Firm match as a player/coach, especially when I scored the winner in front of what turned out to be the biggest crowd in Britain that day and followed it up with *another* strike in our next clash with Celtic.

Thanks for being there . . . and at all those other matches. Thanks for reading this and I hope you enjoyed the trip down memory lane as much as I did.